SMART 2018

The Seventh International Conference on Smart Systems, Devices and Technologies

July 22 - 26, 2018

Barcelona, Spain

SMART 2018 Editors

Lasse Berntzen, University College of South-Eastern Norway, Norway

Printed from e-media with permission by:

Curran Associates, Inc.
57 Morehouse Lane
Red Hook, NY 12571

Some format issues inherent in the e-media version may also appear in this print version.

Printed by Curran Associates, Inc. (2018)

International Academy, Research, and Industry Association (IARIA)
412 Derby Way
Wilmington, DE 19810

Phone: (408) 893-6407
Fax: (408) 527-6351

petre@iaria.org

Additional copies of this publication are available from:

Curran Associates, Inc.
57 Morehouse Lane
Red Hook, NY 12571 USA
Phone: 845-758-0400
Fax: 845-758-2633
Email: curran@proceedings.com
Web: www.proceedings.com

Table of Contents

SMART 2018

Foreword

The Seventh International Conference on Smart Systems, Devices and Technologies (SMART 2018), held between July 22 - 26, 2018- Barcelona, Spain, continues a series of events covering tendencies towards future smart cities, specialized technologies and devices, environmental sensing, energy optimization, pollution control and socio-cultural aspects.

Digital societies take rapid developments toward smart environments. More and more social services are digitally available to citizens. The concept of 'smart cities' including all devices, services, technologies and applications associated with the concept sees a large adoption. Ubiquity and mobility added new dimensions to smart environments. Adoption of smartphones and digital finder maps, and increasing budgets for technical support of services to citizens settled a new behavioral paradigm of city inhabitants.

We take here the opportunity to warmly thank all the members of the SMART 2018 Technical Program Committee, as well as the numerous reviewers. The creation of such a broad and high quality conference program would not have been possible without their involvement. We also kindly thank all the authors who dedicated much of their time and efforts to contribute to SMART 2018. We truly believe that, thanks to all these efforts, the final conference program consisted of top quality contributions.

Also, this event could not have been a reality without the support of many individuals, organizations, and sponsors. We are grateful to the members of the SMART 2018 organizing committee for their help in handling the logistics and for their work to make this professional meeting a success.

We hope that SMART 2018 was a successful international forum for the exchange of ideas and results between academia and industry and for the promotion of progress in the field of smart systems, devices and technologies.

We are convinced that the participants found the event useful and communications very open. We hope that Barcelona provided a pleasant environment during the conference and everyone saved some time to enjoy the charm of the city.

SMART 2018 Chairs:

SMART Steering Committee

Wolfgang Leister, Norsk Regnesentral, Norway
Christine Perakslis, Johnson & Wales University, USA
Brendan O'Flynn, Tyndall National Institute | University College Cork, Ireland
Sanja Lazarova-Molnar, University of Southern Denmark, Denmark
Lasse Berntzen, University College of Southeast, Norway
Markus Taumberger, VTT Technical Research Center of Finland Ltd., Finland
Jianguo Ding, University of Skövde, Sweden

SMART Industry/Research Advisory Committee

Steffen Fries, Siemens AG, Germany
Andrea Vinci, CNR - National Research Council of Italy | Institute for High Performance Computing and Networking (ICAR), Italy

SMART 2018

COMMITTEE

SMART Steering Committee

Wolfgang Leister, Norsk Regnesentral, Norway
Christine Perakslis, Johnson & Wales University, USA
Brendan O'Flynn, Tyndall National Institute | University College Cork, Ireland
Sanja Lazarova-Molnar, University of Southern Denmark, Denmark
Lasse Berntzen, University College of Southeast, Norway
Markus Taumberger, VTT Technical Research Center of Finland Ltd., Finland
Jianguo Ding, University of Skövde, Sweden

SMART Industry/Research Advisory Committee

Steffen Fries, Siemens AG, Germany
Andrea Vinci, CNR - National Research Council of Italy | Institute for High Performance Computing and Networking (ICAR), Italy

SMART 2018 Technical Program Committee

Sukaina Al-Nasrawi, Beirut Arab University, Lebanon
Cristina Alcaraz, University of Malaga, Spain
Ryosuke Ando, TTRI (Toyota Transportation Research Institute), Japan
Georg Aumayr, Johanniter, Austria
Petko Bakalov, Environmental Systems Research Institute (ESRI), USA
Jie Bao, Microsoft Research, China
Karolina Baras, Madeira Interactive Technologies Institute (M-ITI) - University of Madeira, Portugal
Kashinath Basu, Oxford Brookes University, UK
Mohammed Bennamoun, The University of Western Australia, Australia
Lasse Berntzen, University College of Southeast, Norway
Chongguang Bi, Michigan State University, USA
Ramon F. Brena, Tecnologico de Monterrey, Mexico
David Brosset, Naval Academy Research Institute, France
Nélio Cacho, Federal University of Rio Grande do Norte, Brazil
Vicente Carabias-Hütter, ZHAW Zurich University of Applied Sciences, Switzerland
Juan-Carlos Cano, Universitat Politecnica de Valencia, Spain
Raffaele Carli, Politecnico di Bari, Italy
Rosa Cervera, Universidad de Alcalá, Spain
Dimitris Chatzopoulos, The Hong Kong University of Science and Technology, Hong Kong
Yuen Chau, Singapore University of Technology and Design, Singapore
DeJiu Chen, KTH Royal Institute of Technology, Sweden
Seyed Ali Cheraghi, Wichita State University, USA
Yao-Yi Chiang, University of Southern California, USA
Jacek Chmielewski, Poznan University of Economics and Business, Poland
Francesco Ciari, ETH Zürich | IVT - Institute for Transport Planning and Systems, Switzerland

Patrizio Dazzi, ISTI-CNR,
María del Mar Gómez Zamora, Universidad Rey Juan Carlos, Spain
Jianguo Ding, University of Skövde, Sweden
Karim Djemame, University of Leeds, UK
Mariagrazia Dotoli, Politecnico di Bari, Italy
Abdelali El Bouchti, Bournemouth University, Poole, UK / Hassan 2nd University, Casablanca, Morocco
Markus Endler, PUC-Rio, Brazil
Ava Fatah gen Schieck, The Bartlett School of Architecture | University College London, UK
Adrian Florea, 'Lucian Blaga' University of Sibiu, Romania
Steffen Fries, Siemens AG, Germany
Angelo Furno, Université de Lyon, France
Ivan Ganchev, University of Limerick, Ireland / Plovdiv University "Paisii Hilendarski", Bulgaria
Mariusz Giergiel, AGH University of Science and Technology, Krakow, Poland
Yann Glouche, INRIA, Caen, France, France
Katie Goeman, KU Leuven - University of Leuven, Belgium
Jorge J. Gomez-Sanz, Universidad Complutense de Madrid, Spain
Carlos Guerrero, University of Balearic Islands, Spain
Marco Antonio Gutiérrez Giraldo, Universidad de Extremadura, Spain
Carlos Henggeler Antunes, University of Coimbra, Portugal
Pascal Hirmer, University of Stuttgart, Germany
Gerold Hoelzl, University of Passau, Germany
Tzung-Pei Hong, National University of Kaohsiung, Taiwan
Maysoun Ibrahim, Beirut Arab University, Lebanon
Sergio Ilarri, University of Zaragoza, Spain
Ming Jin, UC Berkeley / LBNL, USA
Bilal Kartal, University of Minnesota, USA
Abdelmajid Khelil, Landshut University of Applied Sciences, Germany
Pinar Kirci, Istanbul University, Turkey
Francine Krief, Bordeaux INP, France
Kirill Krinkin, Saint-Petersburg Electrotechnical University, Russia
Sanja Lazarova-Molnar, University of Southern Denmark, Denmark
Wolfgang Leister, Norsk Regnesentral, Norway
Dan Lin, Missouri University of Science and Technology, USA
Giovanni Livraga, Università degli Studi di Milano, Italy
Tatiana K. Madsen, Aalborg University, Denmark
Francisco Martins, University of Lisbon, Portugal
Renato Martins, INRIA | Sophia Antipolis, France
Manuel Mastrofini, LAST Horizon / University of Rome Tor Vergata, Italy
Natarajan Meghanathan, Jackson State University, USA
Zahéra Mekkioui, University of Tlemcen, Algeria
Jolanta Mizera-Pietraszko, Institute of Mathematics and Informatics | Opole University, Poland
Young Moon, Syracuse University, USA
Matteo Mordacchini, IIT-CNR,
Helena Nadais, CESAM - Centre for Environmental and Marine Studies | University of Aveiro, Portugal
Dmitry Namiot, Lomonosov Moscow State University, Russia
Ulrich Norbisrath, University of Applied Sciences Upper Austria (FH UA) Linz, Austria / George Mason University, USA
Carlo Alberto Nucci, University of Bologna, Italy

Brendan O'Flynn, Tyndall National Institute | University College Cork, Ireland
Edoardo Patti, Politecnico di Torino, Italy
Luis Paulo Reis, University of Minho, Portugal
Jun Peng, University of Texas - Rio Grande Valley, USA
Wilma Penzo, DISI - University of Bologna, Italy
Cathryn Peoples, The Open University, UK
Christine Perakslis, Johnson & Wales University, USA
Nuno Pereira, School of Engineering of the Polytechnic of Porto, Portugal
Jorge Luis Perez Medina, Universidad de Las Americas at Quito, Ecuador
Marco Polignano, University of Bari Aldo Moro, Italy
Heng Qi, Dalian University of Technology, China
Sherif Rashad, University of Southern Indiana, USA
Jose M. Reyes Alamo, CUNY - New York City College of Technology, USA
Michele Risi, University of Salerno, Italy
Enrique Romero-Cadaval, University of Extremadura, Spain
Alessandra Russo, Imperial College London, UK
Demetrios Sampson, Curtin University, Australia
Saiph Savage, West Virginia University, USA
Michael Sheng, Macquarie University, Australia
Farhan Siddiqui, Walden University, USA
Steffen Späthe, Friedrich Schiller University Jena, Germany
Georgios Stylianou, Accenture, Netherlands
Young-Joo Suh, POSTECH, Korea
Markus Taumberger, VTT Technical Research Center of Finland Ltd., Finland
Athanasios Tsanas, University of Edinburgh / University of Oxford, UK
Andrea Vinci, CNR - National Research Council of Italy | Institute for High Performance Computing and Networking (ICAR), Italy
Konstantinos Votis, Information Technologies Institute | Centre for Research and Technology Hellas, Thessaloniki, Greece
Ouri Wolfson, University of Illinois, USA
Pete Woznowski, University of Bristol, UK
Mudasser F. Wyne, National University, USA
Xinggang Yan, University of Kent, UK
Chia-Hung Yeh, National Sun Yat-sen University, Taiwan
Wuyi Yue, Konan University, Kobe, Japan
Sherali Zeadally, University of Kentucky, USA
Petros Zerfos, IBM T.J. Watson Research Center, USA
Bo Zhou, German Research Center for Artificial Intelligence, Kaiserslautern, Germany
Yanmin Zhu, Shanghai Jiao Tong University, China
Sotirios Ziavras, New Jersey Institute of Technology, USA

Copyright Information

A Study on the Application Service for Effective Disaster Management based on BIM

Ji-eun Kim
Multi-Disaster Countermeasures Organization
Korea Institute of Civil engineering and Building Technology
Gyeonggi-Do, South Korea
e-mail: jekim@kict.re.kr

Chang-hee Hong
Multi-Disaster Countermeasures Organization
Korea Institute of Civil engineering and Building Technology
Gyeonggi-Do, South Korea
e-mail: chhong@kict.re.kr

***Abstract*— Recently, because of the continuous occurrence of various disasters, such as fires, earthquakes, and flooding at Korea and abroad, the periodic and systemic disaster management has become more important than ever. For effective disaster management, facilities should be managed through periodic inspection and regular maintenance on a daily, and also in an emergency, the accurate and rapid communication is essential reflecting the situation. The Building Information Modeling (BIM) technology can handle a whole building property data related the specific purpose by using the effective 3D visualization model. It can be used for various management with objects including sensors, Closed Circuit Television (CCTV), which are set in a building. Thus, this study investigates and analyzes several cases of domestic and overseas disaster management based on BIM for effective disaster response. Then, we present disaster management scenarios for daily/emergency/inspection and proposed the detailed data definitions for the application services.**

Keywords-Building Information Modeling; Disaster management; Facility management;

I. INTRODUCTION

The importance of maintenance and management has been highlighted as a systematic daily preparedness requirement, which must be performed periodically, as an emergency response. It is preferred to the introduction and construction of simple disaster facilities, as the aftermath of the recent disaster cases, such as London high-rise building fire, domestic Dongtan high-rise building complex fire, Busan tsunami, Gyeongju earthquake. The Building Information Modeling (BIM) technology manages a building not only single objects, but also it collects the entire property data of the building by using effective 3D visualization model. This makes the BIM suitable for various purposes from the planning stage of the building to its design-structure-completion stages, and even be used for building maintenance and management after the construction.

The functions of a BIM-based facility maintenance system are designed according to the management needs of a landlord or a manager for various maintenance requirements and, accordingly, the BIM data for maintenance and management are typically handled by using a BIM model designed for room lighting to room-floor-building depending on the Level of Detail (LOD). BIM model for disaster management of buildings has numerous factors to be intensively managed, such as major objects including existing extensive maintenance BIM data, essential requirements for disaster management, Mechanical Electronic Plumbing (MEP), and evacuation-related facilities depending on the use and management, or their purposes.

Particularly, the visualization of the intuitive three-dimensional model that can cope with disaster situations quickly and accurately, and the presentation of the necessary information, are the key factors. These are preferred to the spectacular and tremendous information presentation when an emergency occurs. From the viewpoint of fire control, the information, such as the internal structure of the building, the evacuation floor, the evacuation staircase, the number of floors, and the entrance are major items that allow a clear judgment in an urgent situation. Furthermore, such information can provide intuitive understanding in visualizing evacuation routes and planning based on floor structure and scenario. For this purpose, the tasks, which require building information, such as property information and 3D models, should be identified.

Thus, this study investigated and analyzed disaster Facility Management (FM) cases with BIM at domestic and overseas in Section 2. In Section 3, the facility management systems are analyzed and the utilized service and data are defined. In Section 4, BIM-based disaster management services are proposed as daily / emergency / inspection scenarios.

II. RESEARCH ANALYSIS

Recent studies on disaster management and response have suggested effective measures in terms of minimizing the spread of disasters. As the necessity of disaster management using three-dimensional data has recently emerged, various studies on pre-/post-utilization methods have been conducted. In this chapter, the domestic and overseas research trends on disaster management using BIM are examined.

Bin Wang et al. [1] reported on issues, such as fire evacuation simulation and various evacuation routes, which are mainly mentioned in the emergency management field of buildings, through BIM-based virtual environment, which is widely used in the Virtual Reality (VR) technology and game engine. Drogemuller Robin [2] presented a method to support pre-simulation of occupant behavior and building operation in regular and emergency situations by using physical virtual objects including the space of 3D BIM model. Jung-Hoon Han, et al. [3] studied the developmental direction of the active integrated disaster prevention system using 3D shape visualization by applying BIM technology to build situation management and response framework required for active disaster management. Byung-cheol Gong, et al. [4] developed a fire control module to solve the problems of the high-cost installation system having only the simple alarm function, and constructed a preventive system capable of performing self-diagnosis check, initial suppression, and fire-fighting information management. Geon-Hyung Lee [5] proposed the effects and utilization of BIM in terms of quality/cost/process/safety/environment when installing BIM in the fire prevention and disaster field through construction, utilization and monitoring of BIM DB. Eun-Ho Oh, et al. [6] presented a conceptual framework of real-time facility disaster management system based on spatial information by linking to BIM and sensor information model at buildings.

Although previous studies have focused on disaster management systems using 3D visualization and location information of sensors for facility disaster management, BIM data were used for conceptual simulation or simple visualization in the prevention aspect. Thus, this study analyzes various existing domestic disaster management cases and suggests maintenance services and utilization scenarios capable of effective response using BIM for effective facility disaster management.

III. Overview of BIM-based Facility Disaster Management

A. Multi-Disaster Definition

Among various natural and social disasters, the study defined the earthquake, fire, and flooding that had recently gained much attention in Korea as the subjects of complex disasters. The number of earthquakes in Korea, including the Gyeongju earthquake (magnitude 5.8) on September 12, 2016, has been increasing. These earthquakes caused huge casualties and economic losses over a wide range of areas, resulting in national disasters, including paralysis of the national nervous network. In addition, major fires in the past 3 years and the Busan tsunami have required improvement of existing systems and development of new technologies. This study develops an integrated disaster data platform utilizing 3D BIM data with experts in earthquake, fire and flooding fields to build a digital twin-type facility disaster management system that can be effectively addressed. It is intended to be established of response strategy for multi-disaster, and advanced disaster response system centered around the integrated control tower.

B. Facility Management System Analysis and Function Definition

This study investigated and analyzed domestic and overseas facility management systems to define BIM infrastructure disaster management functions. The BIM-based facility disaster management proposed in this study should be able to manage the overall facility and to respond to needs through an integrated system in case of an emergency. In this case, the management system should receive the data from real-time/non-real-time sensors, recognize the situation, confirm the more accurate situation with Closed Circuit Television (CCTV), and respond to the situation through use of the proper firefighting facilities, which are all required for effective disaster management system.

Typically, the facility management system consists of basic information inquiry, energy usage inquiry, space management, facility management, maintenance, and event alarms [7]. In case of a disaster, the monitoring system is constructed based on the detection of the initial situation using CCTV [8]. This is the level at which managers use the primary CCTV equipment to judge and respond to the situation. A more specialized system is composed of functions, such as notification of sensor data and real-time monitoring data based on spatial information about the location of occurrence, by linking to sensors and system for detecting the initial situation [9].

Figure 1. Process of facility disaster management service derivation

Through a BIM-based facility management service derivation process, as shown in Figure 1, this study categorized main functions to be proposed by using the BIM data among various similar services obtained from the above examples, in terms of 1) facility information management area, 2) 3D visualization area, and 3) disaster management area.

- FM- A single system was formed by the division of functional units, such as space management, energy management, cost management, etc.
- 3D visualization - 3D model object control method differs by each system. / 2D/3D conversion mode is required depending on the function. / There are various ways to represent attribute information, such as pop-ups and tooltips.
- Disaster Control - Visual effect methods of notifying the disaster occurrence space are diverse (the whole space, icon utilization, etc.) / Real-time notification board is provided to control facilities

C. Utilized Services and Data Definition

This study limited the utilized service target to high-rise and complex facilities that are easier to manage within the environment, as well as to information management of facility disaster management system. Furthermore, a consultation meeting was held with numerous related experts, such as the actual high-rise apartment managers, FM managers at major domestic complex facilities and trade centers, as well as experts from the disaster safety industry and academia. As a result, space management and the disaster-related facility management were finally selected by primarily organizing common management functions in terms of facility disaster management.

The space management work is performed to improve the efficiency in using each space of the facility. To improve the efficiency, it is necessary to analyze the BIM-based spatial condition and establish the space allocation standard. To analyze the actual condition of a space, the functional requirements include computerization of drawings, standardization of space (use classification, organization classification, and location classification), and area aggregation by space. The space management system can provide accurate results for this analysis. The space management in the disaster management system is primarily aimed at intuitively recognizing and identifying the situations in a timely and appropriate manner by using 3D BIM data in case of an emergency; thus, it is essential to focus on core fundamental functions in space management.

TABLE I. SAMPLE OF FIRE FIGHTING FACILITY PART OF THE DATA DEFINITION AND BIM LINKAGE INFORMATION

Level 1	Level 2	Level 3	BIM data
Fire-fighting facility basic data management	Facility type management	Fire-fighting facility type	Object
	Detailed facility type management	Detailed fire-fighting type	Object
	Facility name management	Fire-fighting facility name	Object
	Location management	location information	Object/ Space
Fire-fighting facility location info. management	Fire-fighting facility Installation location management	Location info. by building	Object/ Space
		Location info. by floor	Object/ Space
		Location info.by fire-fighting facility	Object/ Space
	Fire-fighting facility Installation status management	Status info. by building	Object/ Building
		Status info. by floor	Object/ Floor
		Status info. by fire fighting facility	Object/ Space
Fire-fighting facility monitoring	Daily monitoring	Fire-fighting facility operation	Object/ Space
		Fire-fighting facility status observation	Object/ Space
		Fire-fighting facility operation history	Object/ Space
	Disaster situation monitoring	Fire-fighting facility operation	Object/ Space
		Fire-fighting facility status observation	Object/ Space
		Fire-fighting facility operation history	Object/ Space
		Location display for situation occurred	Object/ Space

Disaster-related facility management is the task of monitoring the building status in a comprehensive manner by managing the information of each facility constituting the building. Thus, the management of the systematic facility information in a regular manner should be able to respond to emergency situations immediately. The information handled in facility management mainly includes basic data, such as type of each facility, installation date, location information, and management information. This study created a facility management list and service data for sensors, CCTV, and fire-fighting facilities. Table 1 is a fire fighting facility part of the detailed data definition for disaster management service.

IV. BIM-BASED DISASTER MANAGEMENT SERVICE

Based on the utilized services and data for facility disaster management previously created, the BIM-based service for daily monitoring / disaster response service operated in the event of a disaster / facility inspection service for disaster were defined as follows, respectively.

A. *Daily Monitoring*

The daily scenarios of BIM-based facility disaster management focus on the basic information and static data checking of the site including the building. Daily monitoring can inquire basic information on BIM-based building situation, construction information, auxiliary facilities, and floor information on the building site. In Figure 2, CCTV monitoring can analyze the timely symptoms, which looks like the disaster, and inform the suspected area with 3D building and location information. Particularly, in the case of a dangerous area or space, it is possible to construct a floor plan separately for the use as an emergency evacuation route and related danger area notification through a space-based management as shown in Figure 3.

Figure 2. CCTV management

Figure 3. Space management for cautious spaces

B. *Disaster Response*

The corresponding scenario consists of major functions for rapid disaster identification and response, in the event of a disaster, to automatically transition from an existing daily system to a disaster response system. 3D BIM data can be used to intuitively access disaster-detected areas, and the integrated disaster management manager can make quick decisions by using the notification from the nearby CCTV and sensors in the target area. Furthermore, as shown in Figure 4, it is possible to provide detailed and clear information to the firefighting team by recognizing spread of additional disaster through floor- and space-based disaster detection, as well as by using the BIM data on building structure, materials, and facility location related to a disaster. Thus, it is further possible to recognize the initial situation.

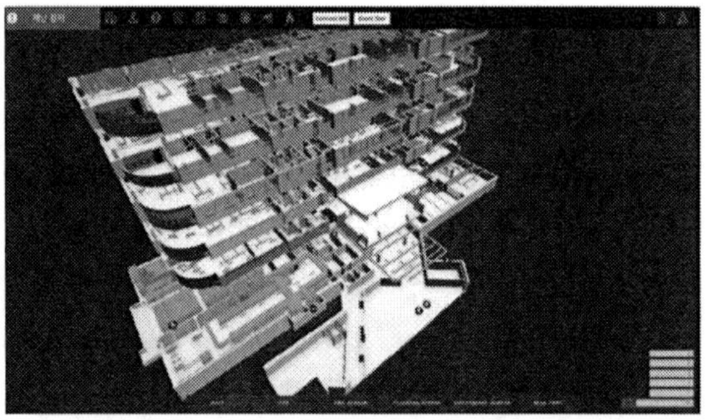

Figure 4. Confirmation of BIM-based disaster facilities

C. *Facility Inspection*

Inspection scenarios have the function for inspection of various facilities including sensors, CCTV, and fire-fighting facilities for disaster preparedness.

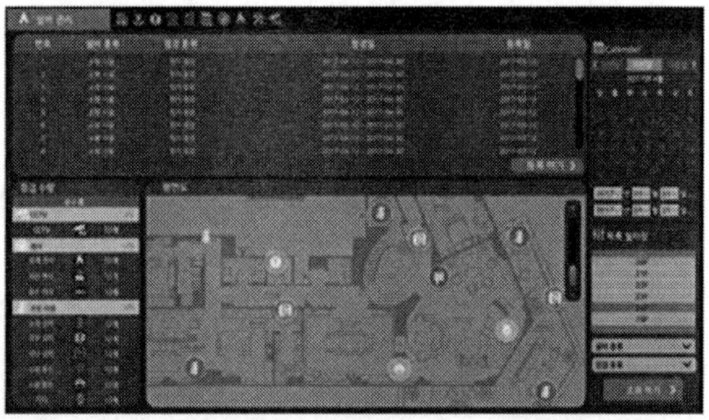

Figure 5. Facility inspection related to disaster

As shown in Figure 5, the facility maintenance team can use the facility location information within the BIM model to establish the plans for daily and periodic inspections, and can manage the detailed inspection history by filtering the inspections by equipment type, inspection date, and floor unit. Sensors can inquire abnormal signals and disaster information history depending on real-time/non-real-time inspection cycle.

V. CONCLUSION

This study investigated and analyzed domestic and overseas disasters cases, and identified the problems regarding these cases to derive facility disaster management scenarios. The study summarized the requirements for effective disaster management through numerous consultation meetings with facilities FM personnel of major high-rise and complex facilities. Based on these consultations, this study defined the disaster-related services and data using the system, along with the necessity for a 3D data-based system for an effective disaster management. This study further presented the purpose-specific scenarios for daily/disaster/inspection situations.

The calamity and disaster field particularly requires quick situation judgment and visualization to intuitively foresee various possibilities. In this regard, the integrated management system can prevent disasters and seek early suppression through daily preparedness as well as emergency response. Future studies will integrate this system with AR/VR technology, which is recently gaining popularity, to build various contents, such as mobile-based facility inspection and management, fire-fighting training simulation, and operation support.

ACKNOWLEDGMENT

This work was supported by the National Research Council of Science & Technology (NST) grant by the Korea government (MSIP) (No. CRC-16-02-KICT)

REFERENCES

[1] B. Wang, H. Li, Y. Rezgui, A. Bradley, and H. N. Ong, "BIM based Virtual Environment for Fire Emergency Evacuation", The Scientific World Journal, Vol.2014, pp.1-22, 2014.

[2] D. Robin, "BIM support for disaster response", Proc. of 9th annual international conference of the International Institute for Infrastructure Renewal and Reconstruction, pp. 391-405, 2013.

[3] J. H. Han, C. W. Lee, S. H. Nam, C. S. Jeong, and S. H. Lee, "Application of BIM technology to active disaster management for flood control facility", Proc. of KIBIM Annual Conference 2012, Vol.2, No.1, pp.47-48, 2012.

[4] B. C. Kong and S. H. Lee, "Design and Implementation of an effective Complex Fire Detector Module", Journal of academia-industrial technology, Vol.11, No.3, pp.1079-1084, 2010.

[5] K. H. Lee, "The methodology of BIM implementation for efficient prevention and response in firefighting and disaster fields", Korean Institute of Architectural Sustainable Environment and Building Systems, special issues, Vol.11, No.2, pp.23-34, 2017.

[6] E. H. Oh, S. K. Lee, E. Y. Shin, T. K. Kang, and Y. S. Lee, "A Framework of Realtime Infrastructure Disaster Management System based on the Integration of the Building Information Model and the Sensor Information Model", Journal of Korea society of hazard mitigation, Vol.12, No.6, pp.7-14, 2012.

[7] Honeywell, Building solutions. [Online]. Available from: https://building solutions.honeywell.com [retrieved: April, 2018]

[8] Anyang-Si, U-ITS Center. [Online]. Available from: http://its.anyang.go. kr/ITSCenter.do [retrieved: April, 2018]

[9] Iconics energy management dashboard. [Online]. Available from: https:// cross-automation.com/blog/industrial-energy-management-dashboards-require-great-toolkit [retrieved: April, 2018]

Contemporary Smart Cities: Key Issues and Best Practices

Katalin Fehér Ph.D.
Budapest Business School University of Applied Sciences
Budapest, Hungary
e-mail: feher.katalin@uni-bge.hu

***Abstract*—The goal of the paper is to summarise the most common key issues and best practices of contemporary smart cities based on a globally selected and analysed research corpus with governmental and business documents from the last three years. The paper also provides a comparative analysis of the corpus with recently published academic sources. The ultimate goal is to create a framework study of the contemporary smart city landscape to support the connected research projects from different disciplines, and also, to give ammunition for policy makers of future cities to their strategies.**

Keywords-Smart city; data-driven society; life quality; mobilisation; smart citizen; artificial intelligence

I. INTRODUCTION

Smart services, products and systems promise that the latest technology is going to force emerging developments and digital ecosystem constantly. The question is where are we on this timeline.

The latest digital technology presents so-called smart devices and smart services. However, our expectation is based on more and more advanced level smart solutions in an intensive competition of digital markets. Our research questions concern a contemporary view. Is "smartness" available in fact, or, do we recognise the early stage of smart technology? Is, eventually, a sudden leap required for a more complex smart systems based on artificial intelligence? Which ideas, issues and initiatives describe contemporary smart environments, from a global view?

Studying the academic sources or professional trend reports of emerging digital technologies led to the identification of two major approaches. A significant amount of scholarly papers have a wide perspective on social-cultural-economic changes reflecting smart technologies and the first developments based on the upcoming artificial intelligence [1][2]. The other massive majority of academic research has presented a zoom into the state of art technologies regarding the highest level of developments and initiatives [3][4]. In conclusion, these approaches point out a non-comprehensive field of the so-called smart environments.

Building a basis of a more comprehensive summary, a short literature review is going to summarise the academic point of view of the contemporary smart city developments. These theoretical pillars are going to prepare the presentation of the corpus-based research. The subject of the research project is going to propose a comparative, two-dimensional analysis of emerging digital technologies with their effects on smart cities based on the most popular business and governmental documents. The first dimension is going to highlight the key issues of the smart environments and the second one is going to present the most cited best practices. Both of them are created by a carefully selected corpus containing the most popular strategic documents or trend reports of smart cities from the last three years.

The ultimate purpose of the paper is to map the contemporary smart city landscape providing a comprehensive summary of governmental and business decision making on this field with an academic analytical view.

The paper consists of five sections. First and foremost, the Consideration of Terminology outlines the suggested approach of smart ecosystem. This section introduces the next one, called Short Literature Review presenting the academic sources. The section provides a summary of a research corpus and its interpretation. The Methodological Concerns follows it to describe the criteria of content filtering, software-supported and manual methods of the analysis. Findings are presented in the next section which specifies the key issues and best practices of smart cities based on the corpus. The Conclusion closes and summarises the theoretical and the research-based results, particularly in context of upcoming artificial intelligence and expectation of engagement by smart citizens.

II. CONSIDERATION OF TERMINOLOGY

Smart ecosystem has been recently defined by building new business, society and culture by digital devices and services in networks. This approach is particularly valid for smart cities facilitated by local governments and business. Following the academic and market-based discourses on this field, our digital environment has become smart, and artificial intelligence (AI) seems to be on the doorstep.

Per definitionem, a smart ecosystem is associated with a place or system highly related to information and communication technologies [5], ubiquitous sensing, data-driven decisions and cognitive computing [6], and optimisation of operations [7][8]. These ingredients determine the design of smart environments with an expected final goal of an artificial intelligence driven ecosystem. The term "smart" describes an intermediate milestone between an initial state of digitalisation and the upcoming artificial intelligence. The former milestone belonged to the coding and the first digital networks. The latter assumes a created non-human intelligence, what is capable to be rational or is able to act rationally [9] and which holds a potential for a good-AI-society with human dignity, governmental responsibility and ethical-normative innovations [10].

Considering these simplified definitions, smart technology supported environments are available. However, certain smart environments still are supported by limited digital services, while others present advanced automated and self-managed developments. The overall picture is therefore not uniformed, moreover, different milestones are represented in the same environments. In other words, digital, smart and artificial intelligence based ecosystems are not available in themselves, only mixtures of their elements are relevant to different goals and different circumstances from the cultural background to the financial investments.

Investigating this complex landscape, numerous news, agendas, top lists, reports and visions are available but a simplified global summary of these is missing. However, a contemporary brief has become indispensable for policy makers and researchers to support constructive co-operations with stakeholders, shareholders and connected research projects. After the considered terminology, this paper targets to fill the mentioned gap by an outline of current academic literature in the next section, and also, by results of corpus-driven qualitative research for an overall and comprehensive picture.

III. Short Literature Review

Starting with the academic sources, the most remarkable summary of smart city approaches is the work of Albino and his co-authors from 2015 [11]. Their research project was focusing on the meaning of 'smart' in the 'smart city' context first. Their in-depth literature review revealed a wide range of smart city characteristics including among others built and natural environments, quality of life, mobility, info-communication technology, innovation, and also, economic or socio-political issues.

Besides, concerning the wide range of academic publications and exploring the highly cited sources related to the topic, the most emphasised issues are the "big data" and "algorithms" in the smart city context [12][13]. Regarding the city-based datasets, the emerging trend is to study the city-operation and citizen-driven open data, and in particular the smart city engagement by locals to share their activities, ideas and opinions [14][15]. In parallel, the number of papers in governmental issues [16] and in local entrepreneurship vs. global companies are growing rapidly with critical aspects [17].

Meanwhile, the technological conditions are changing drastically. According to the Complimentary White Paper: IoT Platforms – Enabling the Internet of Things [18], there were 15.4 billion devices available in 2015. The number is growing to 30.7 billion until 2020 and to 75.4 billion until 2025 with emerging Industrial Internet of Things (IIoT) ratio in it.

These developments are closely related to further rapid changes via cloud, mobile internet, advanced robotics, 3D printing, autonomous vehicles and further upcoming technological trends [19]. In parallel, half of the full population is using the internet and more sensors and machines are getting connected. The advantages of the Machine to Machine communication (M2M), the automatised operations, the networks of dynamic software [20] are measured in dollar billions year by year with direct impact to economy, society, and also, to city maintenance [21]. These trends and numbers represent how the smart technology wires more and more fields of operations and how fast is the speed of emerging info-communication technology via data traffic and digital services.

A smart ecosystem was created recently [22] for efficient operations and for discovering new options for human beings. Regarding the business research trends, Gartner offers a digital hype cycle trend report to with expected technologies in every year [23]. Additionally, Huawei has a Digital Activity Heat Map developing an index of transformation and connectivity [24]. Last but not least, top lists of smart cities by Forbes [25] and further trendsetter summaries represent the strong interest in emerging technologies and their predictable effects in the society and business. Although, these reports summarise developments and innovations by branded contents, an independent approach is also needed.

The next question is how can we improve a comprehensive summary of mainstream contemporary trends in smart technology, which is also useful for academic research and for governmental or business strategies? What kind of key issues and factors force the present developments and forecasts? Which patterns are visible and transparent for a framework study on the field of smart cities? The next section is going to present a research methodology and results to the contemporary smart cities.

IV. Methodological Concerns

Based on the studied academic sources, our research project focused on the latest governmental and business documents building a corpus via multiple filters. The analysed corpus was created by strategic documents, trend reports, white papers, future visions and implementation reports of smart cities from all over the world. Only completed and published files were selected, which were official communication of business and governmental partnerships. The selection criteria belonged to the time dimension and the global representation. The last three years presented the timeframe for a contemporary summary. For global overview, all inhabited continents were filtered and the focus was only on the cities, not on regions or further kind of localities to present a comparative approach. It was a decision to pre-select the most searched documents from the same regions and about the cities avoiding overlapped descriptions.

Based on these criteria, the most popular and most downloaded, publicly available documents were assorted by the globally used search engine called Google. The content criteria required summaries with governmental and business research co-operations. The language criteria assumed only the texts in English for the widest filtering option and for the comparative research study in global context.

Due to the above mentioned criteria, one hundred and fifty documents created the research corpus. Most of them were white papers, trend reports, city reports and strategic visions. Besides them, industrial agendas, local government plans, analysis of governmental-business collaborations, blueprint documents, implementation reports, market analysis, partnership reports and strategic submit documents were also appeared in a smaller proportion.

After eliminating the non-informative stop-words from the documents (such as "a", "the", "or") and the short texts from the visual illustrations (e.g., repeated and highlighted sentences or keywords from the texts), the frequency of key issues have become available from the text analysis. For the common occurrence in a variety of text units the research applied WORDij and Quadratic Assignment Procedure (QAP). Based on Pearson Correlation [26], word connection frequencies and strong ties among the key elements were found to interpret the word pairs and content networks. Gephi 0.9.1 supported the visualisation of the results regarding the key issues. The most cited best practices were collected by the word frequency of the city names and based on it, a manual content analysis produced the short comparative summary of the city reports. The key issues and best practices of the contemporary smart cities in the last three years have become available in this way. The next section outlines the obtained results.

V. FINDINGS

This section will present the general frequency and its interpretation based on the whole corpus first. Concerning the word connection frequencies and strong ties among the key issues, word pairs and content networks are going to be analysed. Last but not least, best practices are going to be highlighted as the content analysis.

A. Key Issues

The corpus of the one hundred and fifty documents presents thousands of pages with hundreds of key elements in a text network. Most of these elements have average strong connections. The goal was to find the most central issues with the strongest ties.

According to our findings, the first strongest word pair is evidently the "city" and "smart" together in this order. On the third place, there is "data" all above of the further frequent keywords with similar strong connection to the "smart city" word pair, which result is closely related to the already mentioned academic approaches. Consequently, all further key issues are connected to the strongly tied central content elements, namely "smart-city-data".

Concerning the corpus results, big data, open data, data sets, data analysis and data-driven decision are providing primarily the innovation, optimisation and creative ideas in the presented projects and future plans. In other words, smart city does not exist without digital data, which is the alfa and the origo of future city developments. The concepts of data-driven society has become a city management approach. The term "information" is also in the top keywords as an extra interpretative layer on "data". Information-communication technology, information management, information security, information governance and information economy are built on the data-driven society to utilise the advantages of the digitalisation.

Listing the further key findings, project-based thinking, service-oriented logic, public issues, developments with strong correlation to research, governmental decisions and financial sources, energy sector and technological concerns are representing the key issues with the highest frequency. These focal points summarise a complex city operation with multiple key functions.

Compared to the academic sources, the role of artificial intelligence in a smart ecosystem is underrepresented and not available in the list of key issues. Neither the technological developments nor the human vs. machine aspects are mentioned in the smart city context.

TABLE 1. MOST FREQUENT WORD PAIRS DEFINED BY PROPORTION, ENTROPY AND MUTUAL INFORMATION

Word pairs		Frequency	Proportion	Entropy Term	Mutual information
life	quality	561.000000	0.000601	0.004460	5.535064
city	design	575.000000	0.000616	0.004556	4.085312
private	public	577.000000	0.000619	0.004570	4.033457
city	development	607.000000	0.000651	0.004775	3.099892
public	sector	620.000000	0.000665	0.004863	4.017711
smart	solutions	670.000000	0.000718	0.005199	2.502526
private	sector	693.000000	0.000743	0.005353	5.297493
smart	development	813.000000	0.000872	0.006140	2.067863
data	city	922.000000	0.000988	0.006839	1.333144
smart	project	951.000000	0.001020	0.007023	2.602895

Referring to the academic literature review in another aspect, the human factors and the engagement of local citizens are more represented in the corpus than it was expected. However, these human factors are also underrepresented compared to the frequency of the key issues. Primarily the citizen-driven open data is highlighted in this context along various sectors and decision points. The focus is on the contribution to the common interests via automatisation and comfortable smart city services supporting the local business and higher standard of living. Engagement by locals or their involvement into the decision making are at least seldom mentioned as a result of the activities of the NGOs, volunteering or being ambassadors of innovative technologies.

The text analysis has also revealed the word pairs to understand the closest connections of the key issues. Beyond the frequency, the proportion, the entropy term and the mutual information have specified and defined the core correlations of a contemporary smart city (see Table 1). According to the results, the "life quality" presents the fundamental category and the goal of the smart city strategies and trends. The "liveable city", even more accurately, a "welfare city" or the the improvement of the city lifestyle are in the focus in most of the analysed city concepts.

The "city design" category on the second place reflects on the ongoing changing status from planning to testing and to the implementations. Besides, several digital services have become built-in technologies or invisible but elementary part of the life quality. The fundamental motivation is the potential for the cost reductions of the city operation. The reason behind the intensive investment to the smart technology by governments and business is consistent to the statistics of M2M in the literature review. Additionally, the documents emphasise the importance of "building three layers together" regarding a human-made physical layer from buildings to roads, a digital layer from maintenance to optimisation, and also, a layer of nature with sensorised parks with monitoring systems and breathing buildings with natural building ventilation technology in a post-carbon city. These three dimensions provide the main constructions of the targeted life quality.

On the third place in the word pair list, "private" and "public" issues are represented together. In most of the cases, the interest of general public and moral or legal questions of privacy matters are not in line. The already mentioned "open data" and its platforms or the optimised operations via these platforms belong to the public interest in a society or business. However, users of digital systems strive to keep their sensitive or private data, and also, control them. In conclusion, the documents in the corpus draw different boundaries between private and public issues as different cultures, technological developments or political systems. In the top ten word pairs, "public" and "private" appear as sectors and their interpretation highlights the "city as an operation" approach. The final goal is to engage the general public to share their data collections and ideas about their cities as local citizens. The above mentioned life quality is the most relevant common incentive in this mutual goal.

After the analysis of the podium finish, the following elements are presented in word pairs, "project", "development" and "solution", what is in line with the key issues based on frequency analysis above. In parallel, the "data city" also appears. It confirms the key central elements, such as "smart-city-data", mentioned at the beginning of this section.

Investigating the content networks, the highlights are different in the case of governmental and business approaches (see Figure 1 and Figure 2). Although the first and foremost component is the "data", it is more crucial for business than for the governmental strategies. According to the corpus, national and local governments are also focusing on the information, which depends on the informative data sets or values. This interpretative approach results in a project-based view in governmental context. Otherwise, the business considerations are more technology-oriented and the energy sector plays a key role in its fundamental issues.

The overlapped fields are the "developments", "services" and the "public sector" presenting the main

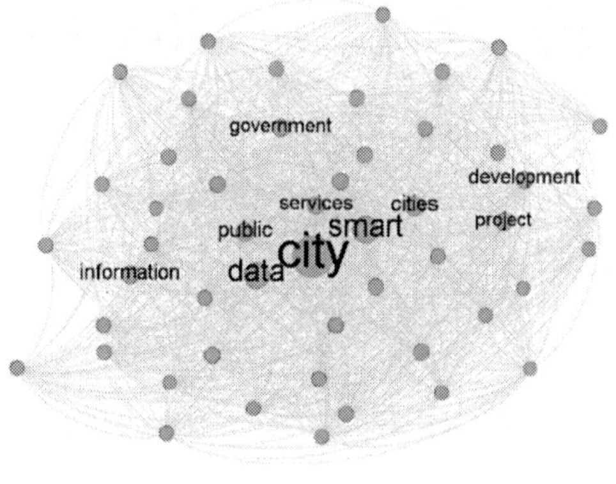

Figure 1. Key issues of the governments in a smart city

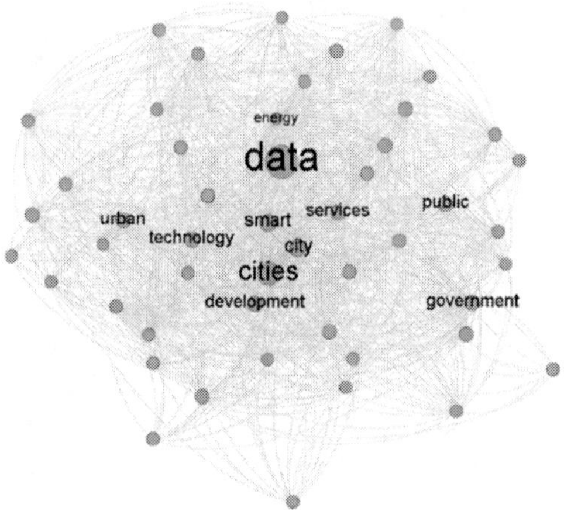

Figure 2. Key issues of business in a smart city

columns of the co-operations between business and governments. Analysing only the top issues, it is remarkable, how determinant is the governmental strategy for the business and not vice versa. This is related to that the framework conditions and fundings of smart cities derived from the national or local governments.

Consequently, the key issues of the contemporary smart cities are the open data, the life quality, the governmental framework and strategy, the capable business to the city design by projects, services and developments. The most sensitive matters belong to the boundaries between the public and private sector. The next section is going to deal with their details.

B. Best Practices

Studying the best practices, the most referred cities are London, Austin, Prague and Hong Kong in the corpus, which is partially unexpected result compared to the latest smart city top lists of business and academic reviews. However, the most searched hits globally presented the following scope, presumably due to the cumulative results of the three years timeframe. All these referred cities have a strong "data" focus with special interest in open data platforms. The optimisation by projects, developments and services are also highlighted in their best practice citations.

Including the highlighted key issues, the profiles of these smart cities present different strategies. The "big data" and "open data" items of London reflect a data-driven decision making in the city strategy, which is correlate to the results of academic sources, and also, the findings of text analysis. Austin joins this data-gathering strategy by Data Rodeo building mostly as an innovative mobilisation. Prague works as a learning organisation using smart e-government with data-collections and also developing a modern public transport. Hong Kong implements also a data-technology hub which supports the sustainable mobilisation and in addition, the ICT-technologies.

Regarding the life quality, the role of the public transport and the optimised mobilisation are highlighted mostly in the best practice cases. In this context, the improvement of air quality is also a fundamental part of these examples, especially in case of Hong Kong. Austin emphasises also the mobilisation issue, additionally with available and affordable city-based services. Prague highlights the importance of sustainability and mitigation of the effects of climate change. Last but not least, London also joins these strategic elements and the city management supports the living labs to test of life quality via new implementations.

Concerning the governmental vs. business supported solutions, the competitiveness of the cities and the data-based governmental-business collaborations are cited mostly in the case studies. Illustrating with examples, the Smart London Board co-operates with the representatives of academic and leading technology sectors, while Prague, Austin and Hong Kong facilitate the local business and the hubs of global companies via accelerated and simplified public administration.

Finally, the dilemmas of the public vs. private sector are less represented in the best practice cases. The reason is probably a simplified approach, namely the mentioned cities presuppose the possible balance between public interest and the individual or community interests. In details, London is open for feedbacks by communities and neighbourhoods, Austin applies knowledge sharing and public hearings, Prague uses digital education or open evaluation system and Hong Kong invites the citizens to smart and creative development services.

To sum it up, the highlighted best practices also confirm the open or big data as key issues. The supplementary common element is the mobilisation in this part of the analysis. An unexpected result is that the smart citizenship with public and private matters is low-represented by the best practices compared to its significance.

VI. Conclusion

The goal of this paper was to map the key factors and best practices of contemporary smart city. Comparing the literature review to the results of the corpus analysis, smart city implementations have diverse patterns in approaches and applications. However, the data-driven logics and the goal of higher life quality are all above. Overlapped fields are the business facilitation in the framework of local government strategy, the mobilisation and public transport for liveability with less polluted air quality. Dilemmas of the public and private sectors can be resolved by improving engagement of citizens, communities and neighbourhoods in open data systems or services.

There are expectations on engagement of smart citizens by the academic reviews. However, this expectation is low-represented and less elaborated in the research corpus. The practice depends on the political decisions, fundings and the calculated cost reductions. The upcoming artificial intelligence should be more represented with clarified distinctions compared to the milestones of digital and smart services.

In conclusion, the studied documents in context of academic literature review essentially draw attention to universal key issues of contemporary smart cities, and also, emphasise on a few fundamental fields, which requires profound investigation before the area of artificial intelligence. Considering the original dilemma, namely where we were on the timeline of digital-smart-AI-based operation, "digital" and "smart" services were highlighted. The AI-based systems are partly available, which starts to support more complex landscape of contemporary smart cities.

According to key issues and best practices, one of the most undigested field is the citizen-based open data and the expected active participation of citizens in the smart cities. The future plan of the research project is to investigate the role of human factors in urban environments from citizen engagement to public or privacy matters.

Acknowledgment

This paper has been written with the support and within the framework of: KÖFOP 2.1.2 – VEKOP – 15-2016-00001 Public Service Development for Establishing Good Governance: The Digital Governance and Research Program. Istvan Boros sociologist and research assistant of the grant provided great help as contributor of the methodological analysis.

References

1. N. T. Buck, and A. While, "Competitive urbanism and the limits to smart city innovation: The UK Future Cities initiative" Urban Studies, vol. 54, issue 2, pp. 501-519, 2015, doi: 10.1177/0042098015597162
2. V. Albino, U. Berardi, and R. M. Dangelico, "Smart Cities: Definitions, Dimensions, Performance, and Initiatives." Journal of Urban Technology, vol. 22, issue 1, pp. 3-21, 2015, doi: 10.1080/10630732.2014.942092
3. Y. Mehmood, N. Haider, and I. Muhammad, "M2M Communications in 5G: State-of-the-Art Architecture, Recent Advances, and Research Challenges." IEEE Communications Magazine, vol. 55, issue: 9, pp. 194-201, 2017. doi: 10.1109/MCOM.2017.1600559
4. C. Rametta, G. Baldoni, A. Lombardo, S. Micalizzi, and A. Vassallo, "S6: a Smart, Social and SDN-based Surveillance System for Smart-cities" Procedia Computer Science, vol. 110, pp. 361-368, 2017, doi: 10.1016/j.procs.2017.06.078
5. O. Melaha, "Citizen-driven dashboards in smart ecosystems: a framework." Interaction Design and Architecture(s) Journal - IxD&A, N. 31, pp. 32-42, 2016.
6. D. T. Larose, and C. D. Larose, "Discovering knowledge in data. An introduction to data mining" 2nd Ed. New Jersey: John Wiley & Sons, 2011.
7. Ericsson Networked Society, "The three ages of megacities" [Online]. Available from: https://www.ericsson.com/assets/local/news/2012/8/ns_megacities_report_4.pdf 2012. Retrieved: 3 June 2018.
8. N. Verhoeff, "A logic flayers: Indexicality of iPhone navigation in augmented reality" In Hjorth, L., Burgess, J. and Richardson, I. (eds.) Studying mobile media cultural technologies, mobile communication, and the iPhone. NY, London: Routledge. 2012.
9. S. J. Russell, and P. Norvig, "Artificial Intelligence. A Modern Approach" 3rd Ed. Harlow: Pearson, 2015.
10. C. Cath, S. Wachter, B. Mittelstadt, M. Taddeo, and L. Floridi, "Artificial Intelligence and the 'Good Society': The US, EU, and UK Approach" Science and Engineering Ethics April 2018, Vol. 24, Issue 2, pp. 505–528, 2017, doi: 10.1007/s11948-017-9901-7
11. V. Albino, U. Berardi, and R. M. Dangelico, "Smart Cities: Definitions, Dimensions, Performance, and Initiatives." Journal of Urban Technology, vol. 22, issue 1, pp. 3-21, 2015, doi: 10.1080/10630732.2014.942092
12. D. Beer, "The social power of algorithms" Journal Information, Communication & Society, vol. 20, no. 1, 1-13, 2017, doi: 10.1080/1369118X.2016.1216147
13. I. A. T. Hashem, V. Chang, N. B. Anuar, K. Adewole, I. Yaqoob, A. Gani, E. Ahmed, and H. Chiroma, "The role of big data in smart city" International Journal of Information Management, vol. 36, issue 5, pp. 748-758, 2016, doi: 10.1016/j.ijinfomgt.2016.05.002
14. A. Degbelo, C. Granell, S. Trilles, D. Bhattacharya, S. Casteleyn, and C. Kray, "Opening up Smart Cities: Citizen-Centric Challenges and Opportunities from GIScience" International Journal of Geo-Information, vol. 5, issue 2, 16, 2016, doi: 10.3390/ijgi5020016
15. F. Salim, F. "Urban computing in the wild: A survey on large scale participation and citizen engagement with ubiquitous computing, cyber physical systems, and Internet of Things" International Journal of Human-Computer Studies, 81. pp. 31-48, 2015, doi: 10.1016/j.ijhcs.2015.03.003
16. A. Meijer, and M. P. R. Bolivar, "Governing the smart city: A review of the literature on smart urban governance" International Review of Administrative Sciences, vol. 82, issue 2, pp. 392–408, 2015, doi: 10.1177/0020852314564308
17. R. G. Hollands, "Critical interventions into the corporate smart city" Cambridge Journal of Regions, Economy and Society, vol. 8, issue, 1, pp. 61-77, 2015, doi: 10.1093/cjres/rsu011
18. IHS Markit, "Complimentary White Paper: IoT Platforms - Enabling the Internet of Things" [Online]. Available from: https://www.ihs.com/Info/0416/internet-of-things.html 2016. Retrieved: 3 June 2018.
19. McKinsey and Company, "Internet of Things" [Online]. Available from: http://www.mckinsey.com/global-themes/internet-of-things. 2016. Retrieved: 3 June 2018.
20. B. Edson by Microsoft, "Creating the internet of your things." [Online]. Available from: www.InternetOfYourThings.com by Microsoft, 2015. Retrieved: 3 June 2018.
21. McKinsey and Company, "The internet of things: Mapping the value beyond the hype" [Online]. Available from: http://www.mckinsey.com/insights/business_technology 2015. Retrieved: 3 June 2018.
22. S. B. Letaifa, "How to strategize smart cities: Revealing the SMART model", Journal of Business Research, vol. 68, issue 7, pp. 1414-1419, 2015, doi: 10.1016/j.jbusres.2015.01.024
23. Gartner Hype Cycle, [Online]. Available from: https://www.gartner.com/technology/research/methodologies/hype-cycle.jsp Retrieved: 3 June 2018.
24. Huawei Digital Economy Heat Map, [Online]. Available from: http://www.huawei.com/minisite/gci/en/index.html Retrieved: 3 June 2018.
25. Top Smart City Rankings, [Online]. Available also from: https://www.forbes.com/sites/iese/2017/05/31/the-smartest-cities-in-the-world-for-2017/ OR https://www.forbes.com/sites/chynes/2017/11/10/singapore-ranks-as-one-of-the-top-smart-cities-in-the-world/#4e260802717d (the latest ones). Retrieved: 3 June 2018.
26. M. L. Patten and M. Newhart (2018) Understanding Research Methods. 10th Ed. New York. London: Routledge.

Citizens as Sensors

Human Sensors as a Smart City Data Source

Lasse Berntzen,
Marius Rohde Johannesen
School of Business
University of South-Eastern Norway
Horten, Norway
e-mail: lasse.berntzen@usn.no
marius.johannessen@usn.no

Stephan Böhm
Department of Media Management
Rheinmain University
of Applied Sciences
Wiesbaden, Germany
e-mail: stephan.boehm@hs-rm.de

Christian Weber,
Roberto Morales
ELW (Entsorgungsbetriebe der
Landeshauptstadt Wiesbaden)
Wiesbaden, Germany
e-mail: christian.weber@elw.de,
roberto.morales@elw.de

***Abstract*—This paper discusses how citizens can play the role of sensors, using their perceptions to discover and report problems using some kind of digital platform. The use of human sensors is connected to the concept of "smart cities". After a literature review, the paper presents two platforms and their use in detail: "FixMyStreet" and "Sauberes Wiesbaden". The two case examples are used to discuss the concept of human sensors in further detail. The paper concludes with proposals for further research on the topic presented.**

Keywords-citizens as sensors; human sensors, fixmystreet, Sauberes Wiesbaden, smart cities.

I. Introduction

Research on electronic participation has mainly focused on political participation as some form of discourse- and text-based deliberation [1]. But citizens may participate in other capacities, as experts (sharing their competence) and as volunteers (sharing their time) or both.

This paper focuses on citizens as sensors. Citizens collect data using their own senses and make an action to report their observations, but they can also be sensor platforms by carrying sensors around. We define a "human sensor" as a citizen that helps collect data about his/her surroundings. Citizens may also collect data about themselves, such as health condition data, sleep pattern data, or physical activity data, but such activities are outside the scope of this paper.

The concept of "citizens as sensors" is closely connected to crowdsourcing and crowdsensing. Crowdsourcing implies that a (large) crowd works on solving a problem, while crowdsensing focus on observations made by a (large) crowd. Citizen observatories are projects where citizens observe and report. This paper focuses on the sensor activities of the individual, not as a larger crowd.

The rest of the paper is structured as follows. Section II presents results of a literature review on citizens as sensors. Section III uses two specific case examples to show how human sensors can be supported by digital platforms. Section IV discusses the findings, while Section V provides the conclusions and plans for future work.

II. Literature Review

The main inspiration for our research on "human sensors" came from Villatoro and Nin [2]. The authors presented a vision of citizen sensor networks based on two different scenarios: Tracking citizens as passive entities to understand and optimize smart city functions, and citizens as active entities motivated by their common sense and using their mobile device to communicate the sensed sample.

Berntzen and Johannessen [3] introduced "citizens as sensors" as part of a discussion on the role of citizens in the smart city. This paper focused on political participation, but also discussed other possible roles, such as "human sensors".

Gil, Cortés-Cediel and Cantador [4] also discussed various forms of citizen participation in smart cities, including examples where citizens collect data to inform their government. They use FixMyStreet as one of their examples.

A search for literature on projects relying on data collected from citizens provided examples from public transport, smart parking, air quality monitoring, waste reporting, urban planning and development, and crisis/emergency response. The following subsections provide insight into how citizens act as sensors.

A. Public Transport

Holleis et al., described Tripzoom [5], an application implementing a new approach to urban mobility management and developed as part of the European FP7 project "Sustainable Social Network Services for Transport" (SUNSET)". Citizens shared personal mobility patterns, optimized their mobility needs using recommendation and personalized traffic services from the city authority, shared travel-related information with buddies on social networks and got rewarded for sustainable behavior. The authors point out the opportunities for city authorities to obtain detailed mobility profiles of its citizens that can be used for assessment of current infrastructure use and future mobility needs. Optimal use can be encouraged by incentives. The Tripzoom app was tested in selected areas in Enschede (NL), Gothenburg (SE) and Leeds (UK) [6]. The Tripzoom app was offering the following value proposition to its users [6]:

- *Be informed.* Tripzoom shows exactly how you travel. Where, when, how long and what it costs. Master your own travel behavior.
- *Be smart.* Tripzoom gives you insight into the way you have traveled and helps with personal suggestions to make the right travel choices.

- *Be rewarded.* Tripzoom gives you rewards based on the way you travel. Take the challenge and be rewarded.

Tripzoom is one example of how citizens act as sensors and also directly benefits from information produced by the submitted data.

Tanas and Herrera-Joancomartí [7] proposed a smartphone sensing application *Incidències 2.0*, enabling users to notify and stay informed about incidents of the public rail network in the Barcelona metropolitan area. Their idea was to take advantage of the widespread use of smartphones combined with their sensing capabilities to gather sensory data from the environment and then send the sensed information back to a central data collection facility using cellular network technology. They suggested using the data retrieved from the application to analyze the potentials of new sensor network paradigm.

In Southeast Norway, a consortium of private, academic and public partners developed a system for monitoring use of public transport. The Trafpoint [8][9] system provides real-time information about passengers on buses. Some data is collected through cameras and motion detection algorithms. Public transport users can download an app. The app includes elements of gamification to reward users for using public transport [8]. The rewards can be shared on Facebook. The app also provides public transport planners with valuable information for changing bus routes and schedules.

B. Smart Parking

Koster, Koch, and Bazzan [10] developed "*wePark*", an Android app for smart parking based on citizens observations. Citizens could report free parking spaces, and the app would direct drivers to a free spot. An earlier attempt by Google "*Open Spot*" used the same approach but failed. The authors proposed to use the app to investigate motivation for users to report free parking spaces. However, no follow-up study was found.

C. Air Quality Monitoring

Several projects have used human sensors to report on air quality. The Green Watch project [11] distributed 200 smart devices to citizens of Paris. The devices sensed ozone and noise levels as the citizens lived their normal lives, and the results were shared through a mapping engine. The project showed how a grassroot sensing network could reduce costs dramatically, and also engage citizens in environmental monitoring and regulation.

I Trento, Italy, Leonardi, Cappellotto, Caraviello, Lepri, and Antonelli developed SecondNose [12], a mobile device to report air quality. The authors made the following observation: "*Official authorities use to monitor and publish air quality data collected by networks of static measurement stations. However, this approach is often costly, hard to maintain and not scalable in the long term*". They also argued that fixed station provides "*a lack of accuracy in the intra-urban air pollution maps*". The device was distributed to 80 persons in Trento. The initial use was high but declined over time. The authors explain: "*Users said they were curious in the beginning, but soon learnt the characteristics of the places they measured*". This observation indicates potential limitations of using dedicated mobile devices for sensing the environment.

Dutta, Chowdhury, Roy, Middya, and Gazi [13] made a similar approach by developing "AirSense", a wearable unit to measure air quality. Again, the authors cited an inadequate number of fixed monitoring stations as the reason for implementing their project.

The EU-funded project CITI-SENSE [14] also made a handheld sensor platform for air quality monitoring: "*Little Environmental Observatory*" (LEO). The project also developed a smartphone app to let citizens report on their perception of air quality. CITI-SENSE ran from 2012 to 2016.

Ishigaki, Tanaka, Matsumoto, Pradana, and Maruo developed a mobile sensor to measure particle pollution. [15]. The sensor was tested in different cities in East Asia, partly by mobile sensing and partly by installing the sensor in fixed locations.

A somewhat similar approach is used by AIRALERT, a service provided by CivicAlert, a Romanian NGO [16]. They use a handheld sensor platform "*AirBeam*" with Bluetooth connection to an Android smartphone. Volunteers collect data, and results are shown on a map.

Pan, Yu, Miao, and Leung [17] used a different approach, by using smartphone cameras to detect air pollution through artificial intelligence techniques to determine particle pollution. This solution requires humans to do measurements actively.

Migliore [18] developed a platform mounted on a bike, "*SwarmBike*", to measure air pollution. The unit has a Global Positioning System (GPS) receiver, a GSM module to handle communication, and sensors for barometric pressure, temperature, humidity and a CO sensor. His thesis describes other types of sensors for measuring air quality.

The problem with hand-held units is that someone must carry them around. Several solutions require Android smartphones. This requirement excludes a large number of Apple iPhone users. Users may also be reluctant to provide access through their own phones. It seems that most of the projects described above lasted for a limited period.

D. Pollution and Waste Reporting

The Irish Environmental Protection Agency has developed the app "See it? Say it!" to let citizens report on waste dumping/littering and other environmental issues [19]. A similar application has been piloted and tested in the city of Dhaka, Bangladesh [20]. Dhaka is a major city with challenges related to pollution (water, soil, noise, thermal, air) and waste dumping. The application was tested over a two-week trial period and showed promising results. In Kinshasa, another pilot was developed and tested, also with promising results [21]. However, this pilot revealed some possible issues related to data quality and acceptance from government agencies who were reluctant to proceed with full-scale implementation. All three examples are similarly structured: They are based on geo-location, and users are asked to report on specific categories with the option to upload images and a text-based description. Pollution and waste reporting are also handled by our two case studies presented in the next section.

E. *Urban planning and development*

In Norway, the Norwegian University of Science and Technology (NTNU) developed an Android app for The Norwegian Public Roads Administration to manage and monitor bicycle routes [22].

City planners make assumptions about cyclists′ behavior based on insufficient data. The app provides more accurate information on which routes to improve based on feedback from cyclists. The app also provides information about such things as speed and relative frequency of use of bike lanes. Field testing was done in Trondheim, Norway, and at the end of the trial period more than 50 people had downloaded and installed the app and uploaded more than 100 trips. The collected data is visualized in a web-based interface and provides city planners with valuable information for planning purposes.

In Turku, Finland, the city created a mobile app, Täsä, to let citizens participate in urban planning [23]. Citizens can download the app to report issues or present ideas for development. The app allows users to pin an issue to the map, take photos and upload text. It is also possible to discuss the proposals made by others. A first trial found that this engaged hundreds of citizens who used to app both to report on problems and present new ideas.

Goodchild [24] discussed the concept *volunteer geographic information* (VGI) and used case studies of OpenStreetMap, Flickr, and Wikimapia to show how citizens volunteering and contributing to GIS sites laid the foundation for other human sensor work such as FixMyStreet.

On the conceptual level, Resch, Summa, Sagl, Zeile, and Exner [25] proposed a system using human sensors to capture citizen perception of public places. They model a combination of geolocation, wristband sensor to measure "emotion" and social media mining to aggregate data on citizens' attitudes, emotions, and perceptions of public places. The results can be used in planning processes of new areas, or as input for regulating and changing existing places.

F. *Crisis/emergency response*

Several authors discuss how crowdsourcing of data using human sensors can be valuable for crisis management and emergency response. According to Liu [26], the 2010 Haiti earthquake was the first-time researchers became aware of the potential of citizens crowdsourcing information. Based on experiences from Haiti, they have designed a framework for spontaneous crowdsourcing in emergency and disaster areas.

Kamel Boulous et al. [27] did a review of applications and use cases for citizens as sensors, and mentioned areas such as fire prevention, medical information, routing of CPR-trained personnel to emergencies, drug safety and disease outbreak mapping as examples. They also present GIS-based tools that can be applied to create other applications

In Brazil, Degrossi, de Albuquerque, Fava, and Mendiondo [28] described a pilot study on how human sensors can contribute data related to flooding, a significant problem in parts of the country. Evaluation of the case showed that this had significant positive impact on flooding data in the areas where the pilot study was conducted.

III. Case Examples and Findings

Two case examples are used to illustrate how human sensors use platforms for reporting their observations. The first case is the Norwegian version of FixMyStreet: FiksGataMi. This version was developed and is maintained by the Norwegian Unix User Group. The second case is "Sauberes Wiesbaden", a mobile app developed in cooperation with the municipal waste services operator ELW and the RheinMain University of Applied Sciences in Wiesbaden, Germany. The two cases were selected based on the availability of data for analysis.

A. *FixMyStreet (FiksGataMi)*

This subsection presents our study of the Norwegian version of FixMyStreet: FiksGataMi. FixMyStreet [29][30] is a web application allowing citizens to report issues and problems related to infrastructure and waste to local authorities. It was developed by mySociety, a British NGO with a mission to make citizens more powerful in the civic and democratic parts of their lives. The original FixMyStreet was launched in 2007. The application is location based. The user may pinpoint the location on a map. Typical problems are holes in the road, broken light bulbs in street lighting, abandoned vehicles, broken water pipes, etc.

Figure 1 shows a screenshot of one of the reports, in this case about traffic signs. After reporting an issue, the report is sent to the relevant authorities through electronic mail. Both authorities and users can comment on reports, e.g., that the issue has been solved. It is also possible to see all reports within a geographical area. Figure 2 shows a map with several reported issues within an area.

FixMyStreet is widely used in the United Kingdom, but the software itself is open source and has been adopted by cities, regions, and countries all over the world. When using the application citizens are acting as „human sensors".

Figure 1. FiksGataMi screenshot.

Our research aimed to find out more about the use of the application, including the number of reports, and the content of the reports. The information was extracted from the "FixGataMi" website by a custom-made web mining application, and extracted information was stored in a MySql database, and then grouped using SQL. The data for report recipients and categories is from 2017. The reason is that new recipients among authorities have been added since its launch, in particular, the Norwegian Public Roads Administration regional offices. The sample from 2017 consists of more than 6,000 reports from all over Norway.

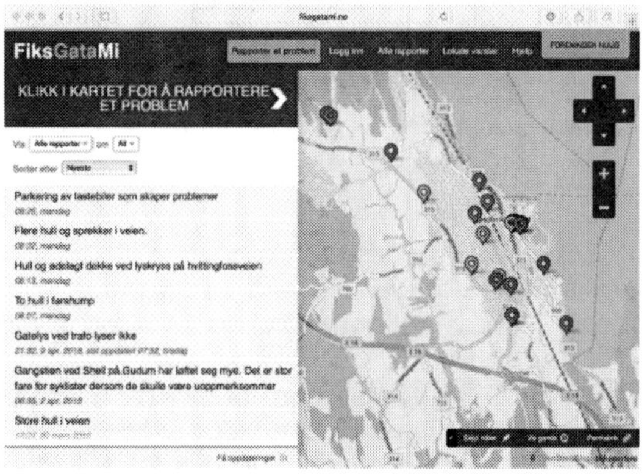

Figure 2. FiksGataMi screenshot (geographical area).

The use has been quite stable since its launch in 2011. The first year had more reports, probably because of novelty and press coverage. Table I shows the number of reports for each year. Each report has a unique id. The numbers are based on first and last registration each year. Some entries have been removed or are reported as unavailable. For 2017 this number is 376, which is close to 5 percent.

TABLE I. NUMBER OF REPORTS

Year	Number of reports
2011	9.751
2012	5.381
2013	6.655
2014	6.016
2015	6.365
2016	6.375
2017	6.932

Table II shows the top ten recipients of reports. Not surprisingly, the regional offices of the public road administration are well represented together with the three largest cities (Oslo, Bergen, and Trondheim). However, also some smaller cities (Hamar and Halden) are represented.

TABLE II. TOP TEN REPORT RECIPIENTS (2017)

Rank	Report recipient (authority)	Number
1	Public Road Administration, region east	2,490
2	Public Road Administration, region west	1,113
3	Public Road Administration, region middle	880
4	Public Road Administration, region south	834
5	Oslo	603
6	Trondheim	490
7	Hamar	472
8	Public Road Administration, region north	454
9	Bergen	357
10	Halden	253

The developers of the Norwegian version added some extra categories not found in the English version to handle specific events relevant for Norway. These new categories are "oil spill", "snow ploughing", "bike roads", "universal design" and "water supply". "Universal design" is about reporting barriers for citizens with impairments. The list of categories is shown in Table III.

TABLE III. REPORTS AS CATEGORIES (2017)

Category (Norwegian)	Category (English)	#
Annet	Other	72
Buss- og togstopp	Bus and train stops	52
Dumpet skrot	Flytipping	44
Forlatte kjøretøy	Abandoned vehicles	62
Forsøpling	Rubbish (refuse and recycling)	70
Fortau/gangstier	Pavements/footpaths	340
Gatefeiing	Street cleaning	124
Gatelys	**Street lighting**	**1,820**
Gater/Veier	**Roads/highways**	**830**
Graffiti/tagging	Graffiti	0
Hull i vei	**Potholes**	**1,847**
Offentlige toaletter	Public toilets	1
Oljesøl	*(Oil spill)*	1
Park/landskap	Parks/landscapes	50
Parkering	Car parking	75
Snøbrøyting	*(Snow ploughing)*	195
Sykkelveier	*(Bike roads)*	106
Tette avløpsrister	Blocked drainage gullies	119
Trær	Trees	116
Trafikklys	Traffic lights	83
Trafikkskilter	Road traffic signs	195
Ulovlige oppslag	Flyposting	4
Universell utforming	*(Universal design)*	13
Vannforsyning	*(Water supply)*	16
Veinavn-skilter	Street nameplates	31
	- No category -	290

FixMyStreet is an appropriate name from the reports it contains. The three top categories are potholes (1,847), street lighting (1,820) and roads/highways (830). Also, most reports are sent to the Public Roads Administration. The categories unrelated to roads have fewer reports, but all categories, except Graffiti, was used in 2017.

B. *Sauberes Wiesbaden*

The project "Sauberes Wiesbaden App" (Clean Wiesbaden App) was initiated by the project office of the city mayor of Wiesbaden and the municipal waste services operator ELW. The project aimed to promote the participation of the citizens to quickly and easily report illegally dumped garbage and other waste disposal-related problems in the area of Wiesbaden, Germany. An app has been developed to make reporting easy and to supplement the existing, previously telephone-based channel for reporting waste dumping. The app uses the location data from the mobile phone to give the exact position of an issue. The mobile app concept was developed through research cooperation between the ELW and the RheinMain University of Applied Sciences in Wiesbaden [31].

The app was developed within about four months based on a user-centered design approach. Project members were employees of the IT department and the call center of ELW, the City Council, and the University RheinMain. The app was to be integrated into ELW's existing complaint management system initially developed for handling phone-based issues reported to a call center team via a hotline. An implementation approach based on a hybrid app (PhoneGap) was chosen to enable rapid development across different mobile operating system platforms (Android, iOS, Windows Phone). The mobile channel for the citizens could not be realized as a website or web app as the technical concept required access to the devices' location and camera. Moreover, the app had to support notifications on status updates about the disposal removal. Implementation of this feature was challenging, as another requirement that emerged during the user analysis was the need for an option of reporting anonymously and without registration.

After a basic requirement specification and up-front user research, a prototype of the app was developed rapidly and used for intensive pretesting. In particular, the localization of waste deposits turned out to be a demanding implementation task. GPS-based location information acquired by the users' smartphones was often not precise enough, reverse geocoding failed (e.g., for green, wooded, or undeveloped areas) or additional information was required by the removal teams to accurately locate the issue. Anonymous reporting was intensively discussed as there was the threat that this could stimulate even more waste dumps or lead to unwanted or fraudulent use of the platform. For this reason, it was decided that all incoming reports are first checked by the ELW team and then approved for viewing on the map to prevent any misuse. A status map was integrated into the app and showed all approved reports and the corresponding removal status. All approved reports can be viewed on a status map. This avoids duplicate messages as a user can see on this map if a specific issue was reported before. Besides, problems reported by a user can be saved on the device in an "automated favorites" list by using an issue ID and then tracked for status changes in separate lists and views. Figure 3 shows the input mask for reporting issues and the status map with the reported issues.

The mobile application was officially launched in the Google Play Store on October 9th, 2015. Versions for other mobile operating platforms followed some weeks later. The initial launch in the Google Play Store was accompanied by a press conference in the city hall and information about the new app on websites of ELW and the city of Wiesbaden, an article in an ELW customer magazine as well as articles in local and regional newspapers.

During the first month, there were more than 1,000 downloads. In this period 469 events were reported. From those, 13% were rejected due to duplicates, poor quality pictures, or because the report was located on a private or restricted area; while 87% were successfully processed. When comparing the app with other methods like calls or emails, the overall number of reports generated by the app has increased by 134% [31].

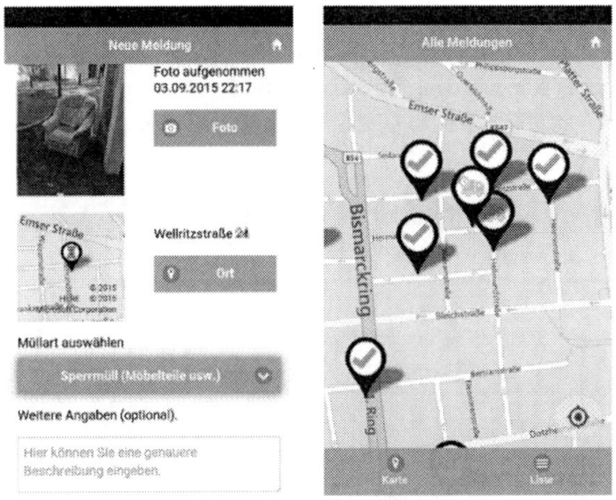

Figure 3. Sample screens of the Sauberes Wiesbaden app.

By the end of 2015, the number of downloads increased continuously. Figure 4 shows the installations of the Sauberes Wiesbaden App for Android and iOS. In May 2018 the total number of installs was 2,318 for Android and 315 for iOS. Statistics for uninstalls were only available for Android. 1,366 uninstalls are reported for the app between September 2015 and May 2018 in the Android Play Store statistics.

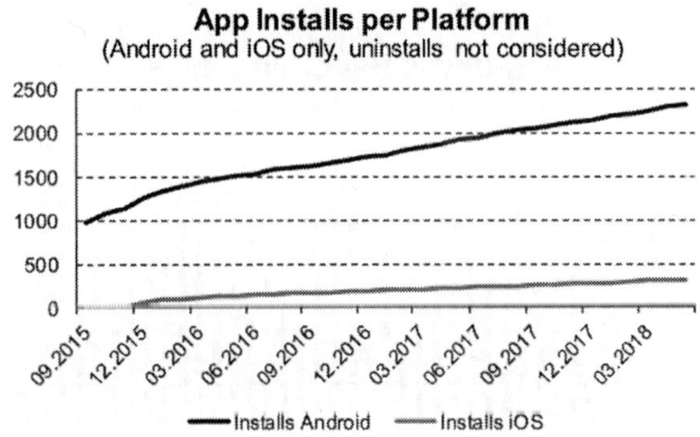

Figure 4. App installs per platform 2015-2018

At the end of the year 2017, 2,154 active downloads were reported via the Android platform. This is a penetration rate of less than 1 percent with regard to the population of the city of Wiesbaden (2017: 290,547) [32] and still below 2 percent, when considering the smartphone penetration (2017: 54m smartphones [33], 82.7m inhabitants in Germany) [34] and the Android market share (for smartphone sales in 2017: 81.5 percent) [35]. A large part of the downloads therefore already took place shortly after the launch. After that, there have been a continuous, but a low number of monthly downloads. This may be due to the fact that more comprehensive app marketing actions (e.g., AdWord or Facebook campaigns) have not yet been conducted. The distribution of the app is therefore strongly driven by references on the ELW websites, the app stores, as well as word-of-mouth communication and user recommendations. Nevertheless, including the test phase, a total of 14,685 issues have been reported since May 2015 (up to May 2018). Figure 5 shows that the number of reported cases is subject to strong monthly fluctuations and that there is no clear seasonal or long-term trend in the total number (app- and phone-based reports) of issues.

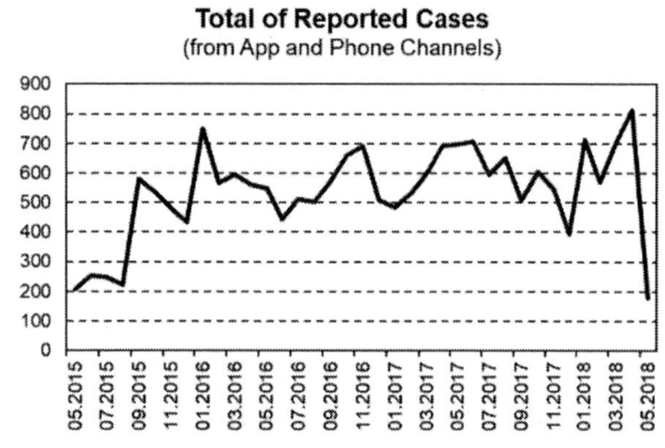

Figure 5. Reported cases 2015-2018.

A similar fluctuation can be observed if only the app-based reported issues are considered. However, in Figure 6 a trend is apparent – the number of app-based reported issues has increased continuously over the last three years.

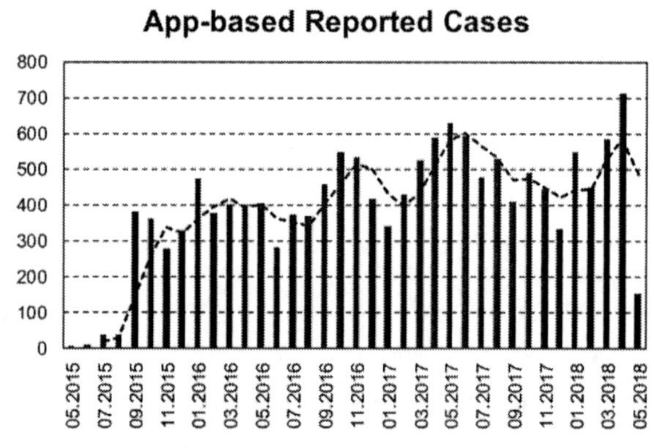

Figure 6. App-based reported cases 2015-2018
(dashed line shows 3-point moving average).

This trend becomes even more apparent when only the share of app-based messages in the total number of reported issues handled by the ELW is shown in Figure 7. The app-share has already reached over 60 percent a short time after launch and has leveled off to around 80 percent in the last few months.

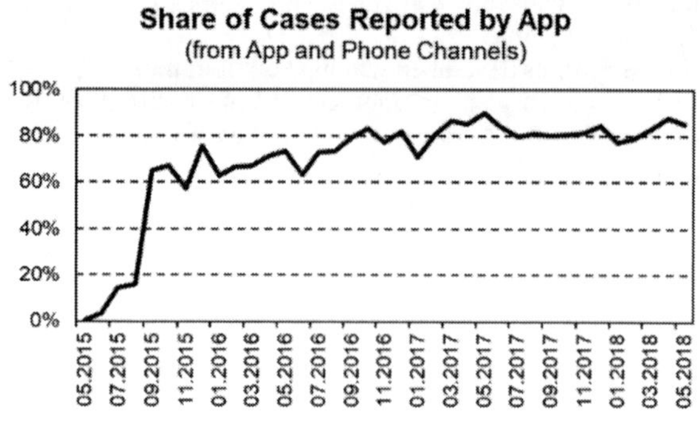

Figure 7. Share of app-based reported cases 2015-2018.

Table IV shows the type of reported issues. Here, it can be seen that a large part of the issues is accounted for by (1) bulky waste, (2) general waste and (3) metal and devices. This seems plausible because this type of waste is the most noticeable in the cityscape.

TABLE IV. REPORTS AS CATEGORIES (2015-2018)

	2015	**2016**	**2017**	**2018** (Until May 1st)	**Total** (in %)
Dog dirt bag dispenser (empty, defect)	10	21	67	26	0.8%
Metal/electronics (devices etc.)	208	662	670	257	12.2%
General waste	315	1,359	1,585	667	26.7%
Garbage bags/ cartons	83	234	221	108	4.4%
Waste bin (full, defect)	34	129	292	74	3.6%
Hazardous waste (paint, varnish, etc.)	38	133	185	64	2.9%
Bulky waste (furniture etc.)	667	2,411	2,729	1,191	47.7%
Uncategorized	68	83	30	64	1.7%
Total (reports)	1,423	5,032	5,779	2,451	100%

Figure 8 clearly shows that the use of the app does not differ significantly in quality compared to the recording of issues by telephone. Since HY2017, however, the proportion of solved cases in telephone processing has been slightly higher. However, this is more likely related to procedural aspects and not to systematic problems in app-based issue reporting.

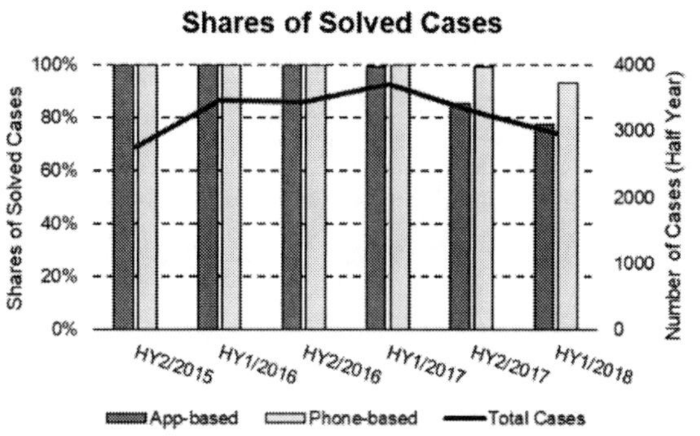

Figure 8. Shares or solved cases (app and phone).

As a result, it can be stated for this case study that the introduction of the Sauberes Wiesbaden App as an additional customer channel at ELW has been very successful. After the introduction of the app, the total number of reported and solved issues has steadily increased. The proportion of issues reported via the app –and thus automatically acquired feedback– has risen continuously. Since the app is available as a feedback channel for the population seven days a week and 24 hours a day, an attractive additional offer for the inhabitants of Wiesbaden has been established. It is interesting that the introduction has been successful even without comprehensive marketing initiatives. However, it can be assumed that the awareness and dissemination of the app can be further increased through appropriate campaigns. Furthermore, it should be noted that the 14,685 reported issues between May 2015 and May 2018 are related to only 2,633 total downloads for the Android and iOS platforms. This corresponds to an average of more than five reported issues per download. In this respect, it can be assumed that apps are a promising instrument to achieve sustainable e-participation of citizens at a local level.

IV. CONCLUSION AND FUTURE WORK

Smart cities use information and communication technology to improve performance and decision making. Data may be collected from various sources, e.g., sensors. This paper has examined a specific kind of sensor, the citizen as a sensor. Citizens can use their perceptions to report on issues. The city can use these reports to solve problems proactively.

This paper examined two specific cases: The Norwegian version of FixMyStreet: FiksGataMi and the German app "Sauberes Wiesbaden". Both applications have proved to be sustainable over time with a respectable number of reports. The two cases were selected based on the availability of data for analysis. We have shown the use and also what kind of reports citizens are making. Both cases provide a feedback mechanism to the people reporting issues, letting them know when the case has been resolved. This is likely important when it comes to retention rates and continued usage of the systems.

The contribution of this paper is more insight into how citizens may act as sensors, and thereby contribute to solving problems in their communities. Smart cities are about increasing quality of life, provide better services, reduce environmental footprint and improve citizen participation. When citizens act as sensors, they contribute to all these aims of smart cities. City services become more effective since the city is alerted to problems, including environmental issues. The citizens participate in improving the city and thereby the quality of life.to improve the city and thereby the quality of life.

Possible future research may include further analysis of the data we have obtained, in particular, to correlate reports to time of year and time of day. Another possibility is to investigate the motivation among citizens that contribute as human sensors. We have currently not addressed security implications of this kind of reporting platforms. This could also be a topic for future research.

Finally, our literature review of similar applications demonstrates several possible extensions to FiksGataMi and Sauberes Wiesbaden: Various forms of pollution, littering and waste dumping are perhaps the most relevant additions based on our literature review, as these are similar categories to the ones already found in the applications. Future research should examine possible enhancements of the two applications.

REFERENCES

[1] R. Medaglia, "eParticipation research: Moving characterization forward (2006–2011)," Government Information Quarterly, 29(3), pp. 346-360, 2012.

[2] D. Villatoro and J. Nin, "Citizen Sensor Networks," In J. Nin and D. Villatoro (Eds.): Citizens in Sensor Networks, First International Workshop, CitiSens 2012, LNAI 7685, pp. 1-5, Springer, 2013.

[3] L. Berntzen and M. R. Johannesen, "The Role of Citizens in Smart Cities," Management 2016. University of Presov (Slovakia). pp. 537-545, 2016.

[4] O. Gil, M. E. Cortés-Cediel, and I. Cantador, "Citizen participation and The Rise of Digital Media Platforms in Smart Governance and Smart Cities," (forthcoming). 2018.

[5] P. Holleis et al., "TRIPZOOM: A System to Motivate Sustainable Urban Mobility," First International Conference on Smart Systems, Devices and Technologies (SMART 2012), IARA, pp.101-104, 2012.

[6] Sunset Project, "Sustainable social networking services for transport," [Online]. http://sunset-project.eu/?page_id=8 [retrieved: April 11th, 2018].

[7] C. Tanas and J. Herrera-Joancomartí, " Users as Smart Sensors: A Mobile Platform for Sensing Public Transport Incidents," In J. Nin and D. Villatoro (Eds.): Citizens in Sensor Networks, First International Workshop, CitiSens 2012, LNAI 7685, pp. 81-93, Springer, 2013.

[8] M. R. Johannesen and L. Berntzen, "Smart Cities Through Implicit Participation: Using Gamification to Generate Citizen Input for Public Transport Planning," In H. J. Scholl et.al, (Eds.) Electronic Government and Electronic Participation. pp. 23-30. IOS Press, 2016.

[9] Broentech, "The Trafpoint Project," [Online] https://broentech.no/2017/11/18/smart-city-smart-transportation-trafpoint/ [retrieved: April 11th, 2018].

[10] A. Koster, F. Koch, and A. L. C. Bazzan, "Incentivising Crowdsourced Parking Solutions," In J. Nin and D. Villatoro (Eds.): Citizens in Sensor Networks, Second International Workshop, CitiSens 2013, LNAI 8313, pp. 36-43. Springer, 2014.

[11] C. Ratti and A. Townsend, "Smarter Cities - The Social Nexus," Scientific American, 305(3): pp. 42-48, 2011.

[12] C. Leonardi, A. Cappellotto, M. Caraviello, B. Lepri, and F. Antonelli, "SecondNose: an air quality mobile crowdsensing system," In Proceedings of the 8th Nordic Conference on Human-Computer Interaction: Fun, Fast, Foundational (NordiCHI '14). ACM, New York, NY, USA, pp. 1051-1054, 2014.

[13] J. Dutta, C. Chowdhury, S. Roy, A.I. Middya, and F. Gazi, "Towards Smart City: Sensing Air Quality in City based on Opportunistic Crowd-sensing," In Proceedings of the 18th International Conference on Distributed Computing and Networking (ICDCN '17). ACM, New York, NY, USA, , Article 42 , 6 pages, (no page numbers), 2017.

[14] CITI-SENSE, "Product Informaton Brochure," [Online]. Available from: http://www.citi-sense.eu [retrieved: April 11th, 2018].

[15] Y. Ishigaki, K. Tanaka, Y. Matsumoto, H. A. Pradana, and Y. Y. Maruo, "Citizen Sensing for Environmental Risk Communication - Action Research on PM2.5 Air Quality Monitoring in East Asia," Second International Conference on Cyber-Technologies and Cyber-Systems (CYBER 2017). IARIA. pp. 11-12, 2017.

[16] AIRALERT website. [Online]. Available from: http://www.airalert.ro [retrieved: April 11th, 2018].

[17] Z. Pan, H. Yu, C. Miao, and C. Leung, "Crowdsensing Air Quality with Camera-Enabled Mobile Devices," Proceedings of the Twenty-Ninth AAAI Conference on Innovative Applications (IAAI-17), pp. 4728-4733, 2017.

[18] C. Migliore, "SwarmBike: an IoT Sensing Platform for Air Pollution," Tesi di Laurea Magistrale. Politechnico di Torino, 2016.

[19] Irish Environmental Protection Agency, "See it, Say it," [Online]. http://www.epa.ie/enforcement/report/seeit/ [retrieved: April 11th, 2018].

[20] A. A. N. Ahmed et al., "A Participatory Sensing Framework for Environment Pollution Monitoring and Management," arXiv [Online] https://arxiv.org/abs/1701.06429 [retrieved: April 11th, 2018].

[21] B. Mavakala et al., "Citizen sensing of solid waste disposals: crowdsourcing as tool supporting waste management in a developing country," Proceedings Sixteenth International Waste Management and Landfill Symposium. S. Margherita di Pula, Cagliari, Italy, 2017.

[22] S. Khodambashi, R. L. Sanders, J. A. Gulla, and P. Abrahamsson, "Design and Implementation of Mobile App and Web-based Software for Management and Monitoring of Bicycle Routes," European, Mediterranean & Middle Eastern Conference on Information Systems (EMCIS2016) (no page numbers), 2016

[23] T. P. Ertiö, S. Ruoppila, and S. K. Thiel, "Motivations to Use a Mobile Participation Application," In: E. Tambouris et al. (Eds.) Electronic Participation. ePart 2016. Lecture Notes in Computer Science, vol 9821. Springer, 2016.

[24] M. F. Goodchild, "Citizens as sensors: the world of volunteered geography," GeoJournal, 69(4), pp. 211-221, 2007.

[25] B. Resch, A. Summa, G. Sagl, P. Zeile, and J.-P. Exner, "Urban Emotions—Geo-Semantic Emotion Extraction from Technical Sensors, Human Sensors and Crowdsourced Data," In G. Gartner and H. Huang (Eds.), Progress in Location-Based Services 2014 pp. 199-212. Springer International Publishing, 2015.

[26] S. B. Liu, "Crisis Crowdsourcing Framework: Designing Strategic Configurations of Crowdsourcing for the Emergency Management Domain," Computer-Supported Cooperative Work (CSCW) special issue on Crisis Informatics and Collaboration. Volume 23, Issue 4-6, pp. 389-443, 2014.

[27] M. N. Kamel Boulos et al., "Crowdsourcing, citizen sensing and sensor web technologies for public and environmental health surveillance and crisis management: trends, OGC standards and application examples," International Journal of Health Geographics, 10:67, 2011.

[28] L. C. Degrossi, J. P. de Albuquerque, M. C. Fava, and E. M. Mendiondo, "Flood Citizen Observatory: a crowdsourcing-based approach for flood risk management in Brazil," In Proceedings of the 26th International Conference on Software Engineering and Knowledge Engineering (SEKE), pp. 570-575, 2014.

[29] S. F. King and P. Brown,"Fix My Street or Else: Using the Internet to Voice Local Public Service Concerns," ICEGOV 2007. ACM, 2007.

[30] MySociety, "Can we fix it? Why you should use the FixMyStreet Platform to empower citizens and open up local government. Version 1.1," [Online] https://fixmystreet.org/The-FixMyStreet-Platform-DIY-Guide-v1.1.pdf [retrieved April 11th, 2018].

[31] S. Böhm, B. Igler, R. Morales, F. Sand, and A. Ertan, "Sauberes Wiesbaden App: introducing mobile e-participation for a clean city project in Germany," Proceedings of the 14th International Conference on Mobile and Ubiquitous Multimedia. Pp. 426-429, 2015.

[32] Stadt Wiesbaden, "Bevölkerung (2017)," [Online] http://www.wiesbaden.de/leben-in-wiesbaden/stadtportrait/wiesbaden-in-zahlen/content/statistik-bevoelkerung.php [retrieved May 9th, 2018].

[33] BITKOM,. "Mobile Steuerungszentrale für das Internet of Things (2017)," [Online] https://www.bitkom.org/Presse/Presseinformation/Mobile-Steuerungszentrale-fuer-das-Internet-of-Things.html [retrieved May 9th, 2018]

[34] Destatis, "Bevölkerung," [Online] https://www.destatis.de/DE/ZahlenFakten/GesellschaftStaat/Bevoelkerung/Bevoelkerung.html [retrieved May 9th, 2018]

[35] Kantar Worldpanel, "Android vs. iOS," [Online] https://www.kantarworldpanel.com/global/smartphone-os-market-share/ [retrieved May 9th, 2018]

From Micro Environmental Sensors to Citizen as Sensors: The Smart Environmental Sensing Web of EPA

Shuenn-Chin Chang
Environmental Protection Administration
Taipei City. Taiwan (R.O.C.)
e-mail:scchang@epa.gov.tw

Yeuh-Bin Wang
Environmental Protection Administration
Taipei City. Taiwan (R.O.C.)
e-mail: ybwang@epa.gov.tw

His-Chi Lin
Environmental Protection Administration
Taipei City. Taiwan (R.O.C.)
e-mail:hsclin@epa.gov.tw

Chun-Ming Huang
Environmental Protection Administration
Taipei City. Taiwan (R.O.C.)
e-mail:chmihuang@epa.gov.tw

Yi-Dao Chiang
Environmental Protection Administration
Taipei City. Taiwan (R.O.C.)
e-mail:yidao.chiang@epa.gov.tw

Ying-Chieh Chen
Environmental Protection Administration
Taipei City. Taiwan (R.O.C.)
e-mail: yingchieh.chen@epa.gov.tw

Abstract—**This article describes how the Environmental Protection Administration (EPA) under the Executive Yuan of Taiwan (R.O.C.) leverages its Smart Environmental Sensing Web comprising crowdsourcing and crowd-sharing [1] built on its existing internet of things (IoT) based environmental monitoring system to make the public care more about the quality of their living environment, and create positive feedback loops of information flows. .**

Keywords- Micro Environmental Sensors; Social Network ; Citizen as Sensor; Crowd-sourcing; Internet of Things; Location-Based Service; $PM_{2.5}$.

I. INTRODUCTION

The Smart Environmental Sensing Web includes continually expanding Micro Environmental Sensors, an environmental quality sensor networking platform, an Environmental Info Push application for smart phones, and an i-Environment website. In Section 2, we also encourage the deployment of sensors, Open Data and crowd-sharing to maximize the benefits of the Smart Environmental Sensing Web. Users may use community links to stimulate other people's concern about the quality of living environment to create positive feedback cycle of data flows (in Figure 1).

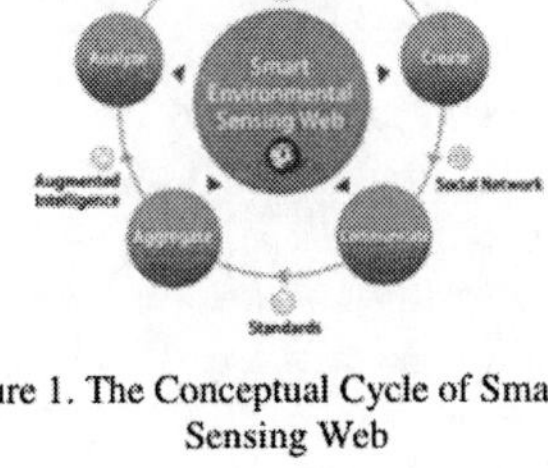

Figure 1. Figure 1. The Conceptual Cycle of Smart Environmental Sensing Web

II. METHODS

A. *Data enrichment— Crowdsourcing*

In addition to collecting and disseminating the various types of environmental monitoring information generated by Taiwan EPA, the Smart Environmental Sensing Network will also incorporate data from Micro Environmental Sensors operated by local governments, educational institutions, enterprises, and individuals.

In order to increase the density of the environmental sensing network, Taiwan EPA encourages citizens to join the network by installing personal air sensors in their living environment, such as AirBox and Location Aware Sensing System (LASS), which monitors air quality that people actually breathe. Since 2016, Taiwan EPA has also continued to develop new sensors that can transmit real-time data to the Smart Environmental Sensing Web via other modes of transmission, such as Bluetooth, Wifi, or Long range (LoRa) [3]. Since LoRa technology has advantages of low power consumption and long range capability, Taiwan EPA has begun deploying these sensors in a certain industrial park.

B. *Technique of implementation*

Smart Environmental Sensing Web comprises crowdsourcing and crowd-sharing built on its existing IoT-based environmental monitoring system, including the continually expanding Micro Environmental Sensors, an environmental quality sensor networking platform with data visualization technology and location-based services to design graphical dashboards and interactive maps enabling users to access real-time local environmental information at any time, while also adding a convenient notification function that sends alerts when needed(in Figure 2).

The Environmental Info Push App provides the public with environmental information that is updated every minute. Internet access is all it takes for people to know the air quality near their home or the place they plan to visit, so they may take appropriate measures to protect their health.

III. CURRENT PRACTICES—CROWD-SHARING

To raise the public's environmental awareness and call attention for sources of air pollution in people's immediate living environment, in the spirit of crowdsourcing, EPA launched Air-Photo, a function of Environmental Info Push app through which people can share a photo stamping real-time air quality data on it, and share the photo on the map as well as on one's own Facebook Wall. Thus, through crowdsourcing and crowd-sharing, the public is engaged as "citizen sensors" and made more aware of environmental issues (see Figure 3).

Figure 2. Environmental Info Push App Air-Photo for crowdsourcing (2018)

The Air-Photo emoji from March to June in 2017 was analyzed and compared with the Air Quality Index (AQI) at the time of posting. It was found that emoji of "Normal" took the most part correspond to the first three AQI levels. On the other hand, when the AQI turned to unhealthy or very unhealthy, the posts of "Hate" or "Can't Stand" emoji had increased significantly. (see Figure 4)

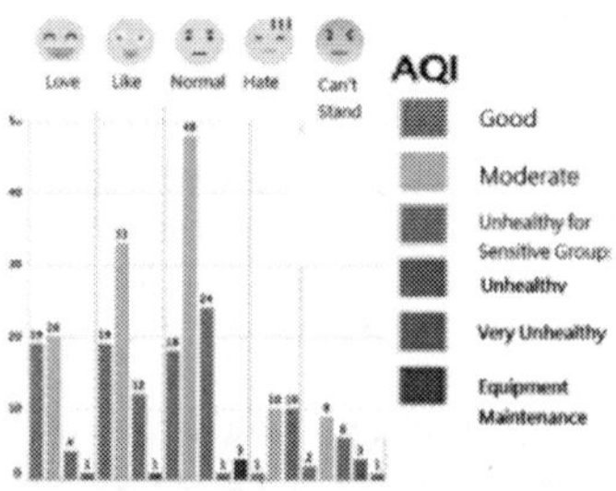

Figure 3. The Relationship between Environmental Info Push App Air-Photo emoji and Air Quality Index (2017/03-2017/06)

Through the analysis of spatial and temporal changes of the Air-Photo emoji and the correspond AQI, it is found the Air-photo were mainly post within the metropolitan areas. Besides, the users of the posters spread from the north to the south and east of Taiwan. During summer, users were less likely to share the emoji with Air-Photo while the AQI were also better. However, when the AQI turned worse, there was a higher probability of Air-Photo sharing with negative emoji among users in central and south regions, while the correspond AQI tended to be the unhealthy to sensitive group or unhealthy.

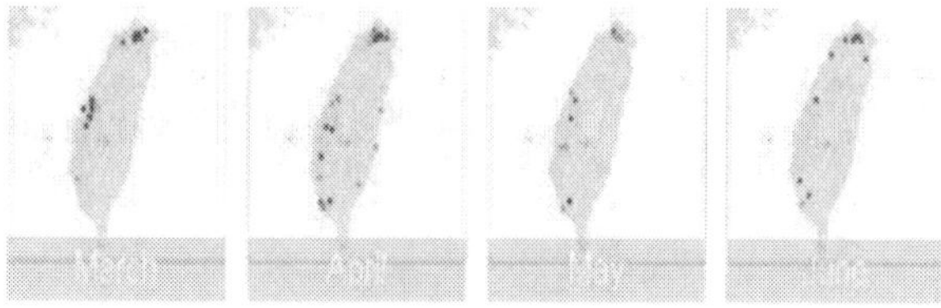

Figure 5. The analysis of spatial and temporal changes of the Air-Photo emoji and the correspond AQI (2017/03-2017/06)

Meanwhile, the northern metropolitan area of Taiwan mixed different emoji levels. Thus, there was no obvious correlation between those emoji sharing and the change of the AQI in northern metropolitan. (see Figure 5.)

IV. USING THE TEMPLATE

In light of the worldwide positive acclaim of Open Data and Micro Environmental Sensors, Taiwan EPA will continue to maintain the concept of open, transparent and innovative applications [6] to serve society with public, diversified, and convenient information services to facilitate people's decision-making that involves environmental aspects. Taiwan EPA furthermore hopes that the Smart Environmental Sensing Web along with the relative apps will motivate the citizen more concerning about the quality of their living environment and transfer the Micro Environmental Sensors to Citizen as Sensors, and create positive feedback loops of information flows

REFERENCES

1. M. N. Kamel Boulos et al., "Crowdsourcing, citizen sensing and sensor web technologies for public and environmental health surveillance and crisis management: trends, OGC standards and application examples," International Journal of Health Geographics, vol. 10, no. 1, p. 67, 2011, http://dx.doi.org/10.1186/1476-072X-10-67
2. IIS-NRL, PM2.5 Open Data Portal. [Online]. Available from:https://pm25.lass-net.org/zh_tw/ 2017.03.22.
3. LoRa Alliance, LoRaWAN What is it. Technical Marketing Workgroup 1.0, Nov., 2015. Available from: https://www.lora-alliance.org/portals/0/documents/whitepapers/LoRaWAN101.pdf
4. Environmental Protection Administration. *Environmental resource database.* [Online]. Available from:http://erdb.epa.gov.tw/ 2018.04. 10.
5. Environmental Protection Administration. *i-Environment.* [Online]. Available from:https://ienv.epa.gov.tw/ 2018.04.01.

Environmental Protection Administration. *Opendata.epa,* http://opendata.epa.gov.tw/ 2018.04.10.

RSSI Signatures for Outdoor WSN Applied to IoT and Smart Campus

Guilherme Lopes, Omar Branquinho, Paulo Cardieri, Eduardo Lima
UNICAMP, Campinas, Brazil;
PUC-CAMPINAS, Campinas, Brazil;
UNICAMP, Campinas, Brazil;
ELDORADO, Campinas, Brazil.
e-mail: g208916@g.unicamp.br
e-mail: branquinho@puc-campinas.edu.br
e-mail: cardieri@decom.fee.unicamp.br
e-mail: eduardo.lima@eldorado.org.br

Pedro Chaves, Raphael Montali, Fabiano Fruett
UNICAMP, Campinas, Brazil;
UNICAMP, Campinas, Brazil;
UNICAMP, Campinas, Brazil.
e-mail: p191678@g.unicamp.br
e-mail: rmontali@dsif.fee.unicamp.br
e-mail: fabiano@dsif.fee.unicamp.br

Abstract - The implementation of IoT solutions in open environments brings challenges regarding the characterization of radio frequency signals, which impacts in the performance of the network. In this paper we propose the identification of radio frequency signal signatures of sensor nodes located in open environments. We analyse the results of a field test conducted in a rural property. For the signatures identification, we employed strategies that use the original signal and the signals as estimated by moving average and Kalman filters. The results indicated the feasibility of using Kalman filters and the original signal to create rules to identify the signal signature.

Keywords - Wireless Sensor Networks; WSN; Link Quality Estimator; Kalman Filter; Moving Average Filter; RSSI.

I. INTRODUCTION

The advent of the Smart City in the context of the Internet of Things (IoT), will depend upon the massive deployment of Wireless Sensor Networks (WSN) in outdoor environments [1]. For that reason, it is interesting to characterize the open environment and identify the particularities of signal propagation, so to work in the development of network management strategies and the elaboration of metrics to be used in Quality of Service (QoS). These metrics will be useful in the preparation of Service Level Agreements (SLA) [2].

In this paper, we propose the creation of a strategy to identify the signature of radiofrequency signals through the analysis of Received Signal Strength Indicator (RSSI) and its treatment by means of Kalman and moving average filters. This work compares these two strategies and identifies their utility in QoS metric creation for WSN. This work approaches the management of autonomous networks and the identification and characterization of radiofrequency signal behaviour for different scenarios in open environments. These management strategies can then be used in the preparation of SLAs.

This article is organized as follows: in Section II, we present a literature review that provides theoretical basis for the proposal; in Section III, we introduce the criteria proposal to identify the radiofrequency signal signature in open environments; in Section IV, we present the materials used for the data collection in a rural property, in Section V, we show the collection methods used; in Section VI, we present the results; in Section VII, we bring a discussion about the results, identifying the pertinence of each method and in Section VIII we, present the conclusion and future work.

II. RELATED WORK

In this section we map the articles found in the literature regarding the scope of this work. We researched for ways of estimating the radio channel for WSN, evaluating the quality of the radiofrequency communication, based on WSN operating in the 915 MHz and 2.4 GHz. In [3], an estimation-based model using Kalman filtering was presented, it is a software implemented predictive filter. In this model, the experimentally obtained data was processed by the filter, producing an estimated RSSI. From that estimation and the system noise (which depends on the type of hardware, antenna characteristics, operating temperature, frequency, among other factors), it was possible to obtain the Signal-to-Noise ratio (SNR) and then trace the Packet Success Rate (PSR) as a function of the estimated RSSI [3].

In [4], [5], several strategies for channel estimation and radio link quality measurements were presented. They went from RSSI-based Hardware estimators, Link Quality Indicator (LQI) and PSR to software implemented indicators, such as simple and exponential moving average filters, Kalman filtering, estimation of stationary probabilities by Markov chains, fuzzy logic, among others. Also, temporal and spatial correlations showing how the received signal intensity varies over time and space and strategies involving RSSI were presented [5]. The analysis over time consisted in varying the transmission time between data packets. The temporal analysis consisted in varying the environments in which the experiments were carried out.

It is well known that wireless communication is sensitive to obstacles, such as people, walls, trees, buildings, among others [5].

III. PROPOSED RSSI SIGNATURE MAPPING CRITERIA

In this section, we present the proposal for the elaboration of a RSSI signature mapping criteria, i.e. how the RSSI behaves over time and space, considering what was said in Section II.

In WSN, it is frequent to estimate the quality of the radio frequency (RF) link as a function of hardware parameters, such as RSSI, LQI and PSR [4], [5]. In this work, the RSSI was the parameter selected to develop the statistical analyses and evaluations regarding the RF link behaviour, as there are many related works in the literature that addresses this metric [5]. In addition to the conventional tools for statistical analysis such as average, maximum, minimum and standard deviation, it was decided to estimate the down and uplink RSSI using Kalman filter and moving average. The objective was to find the signature of the radio signal, identifying patterns considering both the instantaneous signal and the values treated by Kalman filters and moving average. In addition, an evaluation and comparison of these two strategies was made.

IV. MATERIALS

As the farm where the tests were carried out has approximately 78 hectares, the long range BE990 module was used. It consists of the CC1101 radio transceiver, an ATMega 328 microcontroller and a CC1190 power amplifier [6]. The total power is of 26 dBm (0.5 Watts) at the output of the amplifier and the distance covered is greater than 5 km, which was enough for the tests. The BE990 operates in the industrial, scientific and medical band (ISM) of 915 MHz. It is certified by the Brazilian National Telecommunications Agency (ANATEL), and its sensitivity is close to -112 dBm [6]. Figure 1 shows the BE990.

Figure 1. Module BE990.

The sensor nodes were equipped with the DK106 application board. We assembled four Sensor Nodes (SN) and a base radio station (ERB). Figure 2 shows the ERB and one of SN. Each SN relayed to the ERB data regarding: the link RSSI (focus of this work), air temperature, humidity and soil moisture.

Figure 2. ERB and SN.

V. METHODS

The ERB and all four SN were programmed using the Arduino IDE, since the BE990 module is compatible with that platform. For the communication between the ERB and the SN we used the Radiuino protocol [7]. It is a flexible and easy to implement protocol, suitable for the development of applications of WSN. For the tests, we used a point-to-multipoint (star) topology, with the ERB establishing communication with each SN sequentially. Although it is not in the scope of this work, the Radiuino protocol can be adapted to work with dynamic routing, with the objective of covering areas of shading and reaching great distances [8].

The data gathering was done by a central processing unit, using a network management script, developed in the Python programming language [9]. For the visualization of the data, a Zabbix server [10] was used, as it offers a user friendly graphical interface for the benefit of the clients.

The system was set up as follows: the network manager software requested data from the SN; the ERB then, in turn, sent a data packet to each SN, upon receiving it, each SN replied with a data packet containing the requested data. The ERB received the packet and, via Serial UART communication, updated the manager software; the data then was analysed, and the information sent to the Zabbix server.

The system operated for eighteen consecutive days, collecting data. In addition to conventional statistics, such as mean, maximum and minimum and standard deviation, the MATLAB software [11] was used to implement the Kalman filtering algorithm and simple moving average, in order to create rules to trace the RSSI signature. The Kalman filter is a predictive software filter, which objective is to eliminate possible random noise, estimating future values [3].

The equations are based on the propagation and updating of the current state, based in the fact that the future is the present with some corrections and corrupted by random noise [3]. The signal propagation equations are given by (1) and (2):

$$\hat{x}_k^- = \hat{x}_{k-1}^+ \quad (1)$$

$$P_k^- = P_{k-1}^+ + Q \quad (2)$$

Where $\hat{x}_k^-$ and $\hat{x}_{k-1}^+$ are the *a priori* and *a posteriori* state propagation estimates, P_k^- and P_{k-1}^+ are the *a priori* and *a posteriori* error covariance propagation estimates and Q is the state covariance.

The measurement updating equations are given by (3), (4) and (5):

$$K_k = P_k^-(P_k^- + R)^{-1} \quad (3)$$

$$\hat{x}_k^+ = \hat{x}_k^- + K_k(z_k - \hat{x}_k^-) \quad (4)$$

$$P_k = (1 - K_K)P_k^- \quad (5)$$

where K_k represents the gain of the Kalman filter, R is the noise in the module receiver and z_k is the gross RSSI value collected by the Python script.

In the experiments, the state covariance Q was 0.5 and the receiver module noise R was 10 dBm. The moving average corresponds to a sliding window average, allowing the average value to be updated in real time. For this reason, compared to the average, the moving average provides more information about the radio communication since the average value is always updated based on the number of samples in sliding window. For these experiments, we used a sliding window with ten samples.

VI. Results

In this section we present the results from only one SN since those can be replicated to the others. The SN selected was the node 1 as it was powered by mains power generating a larger volume of data if compared to SN powered by batteries, as those had to made use of sleep mode strategies. Tables 1 and 2 show basic statistical analyses: mean, standard deviation, maximum and minimum for the RSSI down and uplinks, respectively.

TABLE 1. BASIC DOWNLINK RSSI STATISTICS FOR SN 1.

RSSI Downlink - Sensor node 1	
Average	-82,65
Standard deviation	2,08
Maximum	-74,5
Minimum	-99,00

TABLE 2. BASIC UPLINK RSSI STATISTICS FOR SN 1.

RSSI Uplink - Sensor node 1	
Average	-79,05
Standard deviation	2,30
Maximum	-72,00
Minimum	-100,50

Figures 3 and 4 show the RSSI after processing by the Kalman filter.

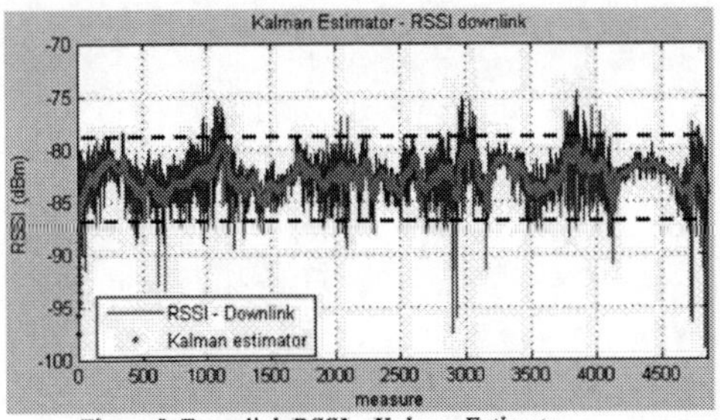

Figure 3. Downlink RSSI – Kalman Estimate.

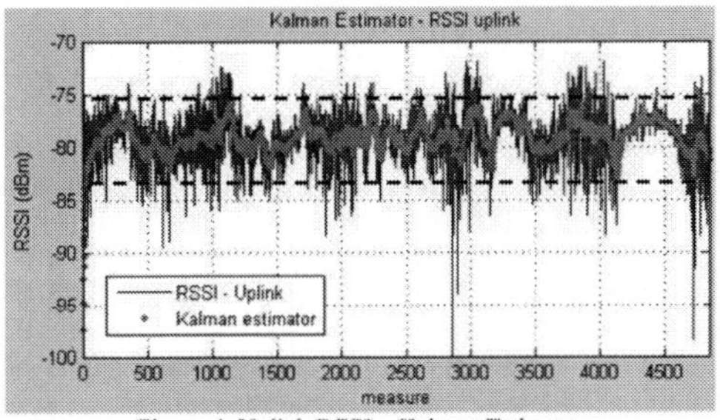

Figure 4. Uplink RSSI – Kalman Estimate.

In Figures 5 and 6, an estimate was made using the moving average. The blue lines are the RSSI original values, obtained by the Python script, while the red lines represent the estimates, that is, the outputs of the Kalman filters and the moving average.

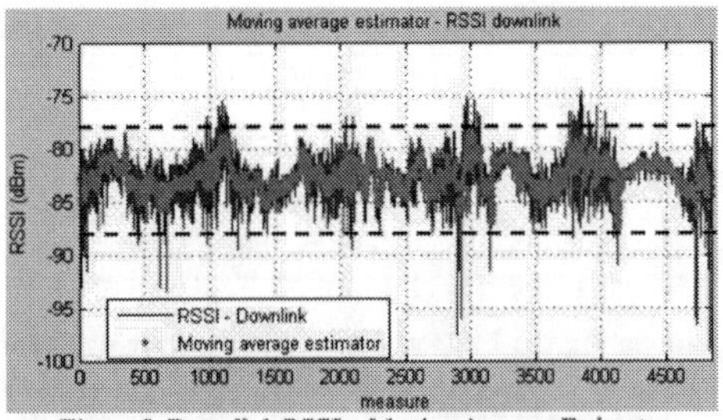

Figure 5. Downlink RSSI – Moving Average Estimate.

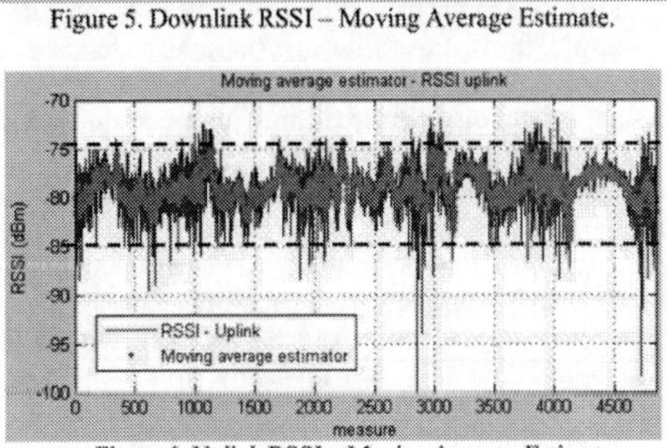

Figure 6. Uplink RSSI – Moving Average Estimate.

VII. Results Evaluation

According to Tables 1 and 2, we observe a reasonable difference between the maximum and minimum RSSI, which can be justified by the value of the standard deviation. When comparing the down and uplink averages, we observed a variation of 3dB, indicating a small asymmetry. In the outdoor environment where SN 1 was located, there are several obstacles, such as poles, trees, motors, electric pumps (potentially generating electromagnetic noise), metal grids, among others. In addition, the SN 1 was located 700m away from ERB, without a line of sight.

Using the results shown in Figure 3, it is possible to observe that the downlink RSSI processed by the Kalman filter causes a smoothing of the radio signal, allowing for the drawing of future RSSI estimates, eliminating possible random perturbations. This is evident in Figure 4, between measurements 2500 and 3000. There that the -100.5dBm point, which was the minimum uplink RSSI value (also shown in Table 2), was discarded in the process, because a just single measurement don't have a significant impact for a output signal in Kalman and moving average estimators. In Figure 5, we can observe that the moving average filtering also generated a RSSI smoothing (in the same way as the Kalman filter), however with an estimate more like the original signal. In both methodologies, it is notable the existence of possible RSSI signature rules, both for up and downlink. For example, in Figure 3, the Kalman estimated RSSI remained between -79 dBm and -87.5 dBm. This means that, according to the estimated value, the RSSI must follow this same pattern and stay in this range for most of the time. The other rules are shown in Table 3.

TABE 3. RSSI SIGNATURE RULES.

Rules of RSSI behavior		
	Kalman Filter	Moving Average Filter
Downlink	-87,5 ≤ RSSI ≤ -79,0	-87,5 ≤ RSSI ≤ -77,0
Uplink	-83,5 ≤ RSSI ≤ -75,0	-85,0 ≤ RSSI ≤ -75,0

Comparing the Kalman filtering to the moving average in terms of efficiency, the former results in a more smoothed RSSI curve, due to the parameter values used in the algorithm. For example, for Kalman filtering, both the state variable and the measured value can be corrupted by a zero average Gaussian white noise perturbation with a certain covariance, allowing for more sensitive statistical analyses.

The moving average is a good strategy to estimate the average over time, but it is less complex than the Kalman strategy, which in turn performs the data treatment taking into account several external factors (number of network devices, random sensor noise, initial values, etc.) [20]. In addition, a decision was taken to work with smaller sliding windows for the moving average, considering that the larger the window, the greater the processing. In this way, it is possible to estimate the development of efficient statistical tools to estimate the quality of the RF link, and then discover the signal signatures in time and space.

VIII. Conclusions and Future Work

The focus of this work was to collect RSSI data from one SN in the network and analyse how the radio signal behaves over time and space. For this, simple statistical strategies were used as mean, standard deviation, maximum and minimum and later, Kalman filtering and moving average. The objective was to analyse the values estimated by the filtering methods and then draw behavior rules to characterize the down and uplink RSSI signatures. Results from this work showed that through estimations, it is possible to draw rules for signal behaviour, as can be seen in Table 3. Future work should focus on new rules to make more precise received signal characterizations, seeking a better channel estimation so to guarantee an improved RF link quality. With information regarding the communication behaviour, it will be possible to develop more efficient WSN management strategies, ensuring high levels of QoS in the SLA of the WSN.

References

[1] N. Khalil, M. R. Abid and D. Benhaddou, "Wireless Sensor Networks for Internet of Things". Available from: https://ieeexplore.ieee.org/document/6827681/ [Accessed: July, 2018].

[2] F. V. G. Gaillard, D. Barthel and F. Theoleyre, "Service Level Agreements for Wireless Sensor Networks: a WSN Operator's Point of View". Available from: https://hal.inria.fr/hal-00998906/document [Accessed: July, 2018]

[3] M. Senel, K. Chintalapudi, D. Lal, A. Keshavarzian and E. J. Coyle, "A Kalman Filter Based Link Quality Estimation Scheme for Wireless Sensor Networks". Available from: https://ieeexplore.ieee.org/document/4411079/ [Accessed: March, 2018].

[4] A. Bildea, "Link Quality in Wireless Sensor Networks". Available from: https://tel.archives-ouvertes.fr/tel-01167272/document [Accessed: July, 2018].

[5] N. Baccour, A. Koubaa, L. Mottola, M. A. Zuniga, H. Youssef, C. A. Boano and M. Alves, "Radio Link Quality in Wireless Sensor Networks: a Survey". Available from: https://dl.acm.org/citation.cfm?id=2240123 [Accessed: March. 2018].

[6] "Texas Instruments cc1101 transceiver." [Online]. Available from: https://e2e.ti.com/support/wireless_connectivity/w/design_notes/calculation-and-usage-of-lqi-and-rss. [Accessed: March. 2018].

[7] "Radiuino Plataform Solution for Wireless Sensor Nodes". [Online]. Available from: http://radiuino.cc/. [Accessed: June. 2018].

[8] R. F. Oliveira, "Proxy Manager for Internet of Things". Available from: http://tede.bibliotecadigital.puc-campinas.edu.br:8080/jspui/handle/tede/898 [Accessed: July. 2018].

[9] "Python Software Foundation." [Online]. Available from: https://www.python.org/. [Accessed: July. 2018].

[10] "Official Zabbix Web Site." [Online]. Available from: https://www.zabbix.com. [Accessed: July. 2018].

[11] "Official Matlab Web Site" [Online]. Available from: https://www.mathworks.com/products/matlab.html. [Accessed: July. 2018].

Verification of Security Protocols for Smart Meters in Smart Grid Networks

Mustafa Saed
Electrical and Computer Engineering
University of Detroit Mercy
Detroit, USA
email: saedma@udmercy.edu

Nizar Al Holou and Kevin Daimi
College of Engineering and Science
University of Detroit Mercy
Detroit, USA
email: {alholoun, daimikj}@udmercy.edu

Abstract— **The smart grids' heavy reliance on cyber resources introduces frequent security concerns. The extensive attack surface revealed by the Advanced Metering Infrastructure (AMI) along with the distribution of sensitive data including; customer information, billing, and control information will provide attackers with a major economic reason to attempt the attacks. To ensure the security protocols between the various parties in smart grid are secure, automated security verification tools are sought. This paper presents one method of security verification for communications protocols between smart meters, a central gateway, and supervisory nodes using the CryptoVerif tool. There are two types of networks supported by these protocols, namely direct and indirect communication between smart meters and the central gateway. Each of these protocols has three sub-protocols: Enrollment and activation, Smart meter to central gateway security process, and key update and exchange process. The analysis of these protocols proceeds in two phases. In the first phase, the protocols were manually analyzed for security flaws, inconsistencies, and incorrect usage of cryptographic primitives. During the second phase, the protocols were analyzed using CryptoVerif, an automated formal methods-based analysis tool. Several efficiency improvements are presented as an outcome of these analyses.**

Keywords— Security protocol; smart meters; smart grid; formal verification; CryptoVerif.

I. INTRODUCTION

Today's smart grid networks, especially the smart meters, have more stringent security requirements compared to the traditional power grid of last decade [1]. This is primarily due to a smart grid offering a myriad amount of connections and thus is susceptible to security incidents. On top of that, new protocols are frequently introduced to take full advantage of available features and resources, such as appliances' operation schedule, incident reporting, and utilizing shared/public charging stations. Saed et al. [2] presented security protocols for smart meters within the smart grid. Before deploying any security protocol, it is prudent to do a thorough security analysis to understand the protocols' strengths and weaknesses.

The proposed protocols were designed to provide secure communications among three entities: user nodes, a central gateway, and supervisory nodes. A user node (smart meter), denoted by U, is an end-entity, typically a smart meter unit that wants to connect to a collector (central gateway). A user node may be directly connected to either a central gateway or another user node. Multiple user nodes are denoted by Ui, where i = 1 to n. The Central Gateway (collector), G, acts as a connection medium between a user node and a supervisory node (Substation). When there are multiple central gateways involved in a protocol, G1, G2... Gn are used. Finally, a supervisory node (substation), S, plays the role of a Certificate Authority (CA) in a Public Key Infrastructure. Note that the symbols and notations used in the above-mentioned protocols have been changed to serve the requirements of the verification tools.

The purpose of those communications is for the node (smart meter) to provide authenticated information, such as temperature readings and electricity consumption, to the gateways. The gateways would then bill the node based on the information received. To facilitate secure and authenticated communication between a node and a central gateway, the server (Substation) acts as a Certificate Authority that provides certificates to nodes and gateways. These protocols are expected to run over the DNPSec [3]-[4], a security framework for Distributed Network Protocol Version 3 (DNP3). DNP3 is an open and optimized protocol developed for the Supervisory Control and Data Acquisition (SCADA) Systems supporting the utility industries. Overall analysis of security protocols starts with manual analysis (phase1) followed by formal verification (phase2). In the first phase, thorough manual analysis is performed on all the protocols, with special attention given to renaming and arranging the symbols and notations used in the three protocols as these notations may not suitable for the verification algorithm. In the second phase, protocols are analyzed using a formal method-based approach. Formal methods-based verification consists of a process for generating a set of reductions that connects the protocol to some known hard problems. It is usually carried out manually, which may require a lot of creativity and effort. This could have a direct impact on the cryptographic design of the protocol. However, modern protocols tend to be more and more complicated and it is possible that a manual analysis may not cover all the aspects. Additionally, human errors may surface during the generation of long sequences of proofs. To this end, researchers sometimes resort to automated verification tools.

An excellent verification tool is CryptoVerif [5]. It is an automated tool to verify the secrecy and authenticity of a cryptographic protocol. It provides a generic mechanism for specifying the security assumptions on cryptographic primitives.

CryptoVerif has been used to analyze a number of important schemes and protocols in the field. Bhargavan et al. [6] performed a formal verification using CryptoVerif and established the correctness of the authenticated key exchange protocol within the Transport Layer Security (TLS) protocol. The authors also provided an automated proof that concluded the security of the handshake protocol within TLS is as hard as the underlying Diffie-Hellman assumption over certain groups. In the field of network security, TLS is perhaps the most important and widely used protocol for secure communications over the Internet [7]. Numerous analyses have been performed using this scheme over the years, in instances where manual analysis is performed to show the correctness of the scheme [8]-[10].

Blanchet and Pointcheval [11] analyzed the Full Domain Hash (FDH) scheme where CryptoVerif was used to generate automated security proof via sequence games. Their analysis showed that the FDH was scheme remains secure so long as the RSA scheme and the hash function are secure. FDH formalized by Bellare and Rogaway in [12] using the RSA encryption scheme [13].

Prior to introducing CryptoVerif, Blanchet [14], introduced another tool, ProVerif. This tool is enhanced and improved to get the CryptoVerif tool.

This paper adopts the CryptoVerif tool to analyze the three protocols presented in [2]. It first presents formalized descriptions of all the protocols performed. This is done by addressing some of the shortcomings identified during manual analysis, such as the translation of the notations used in the three protocols language in accordance to the language understood by cryptoVerif tool. The manual analysis also identified the potential for improvements to the protocols in terms of network throughput and latency. Next, the protocols were translated into the language (codes) of CryptoVerif for formal verification. These codes were then executed using the tool, generating a sequence of proofs that confirm the security of the protocol.

The reminder of the paper is organized as follows: Section II provides all the necessary notations and primitives. Overview of formal verification and CryptoVerif tool are presented in Section III. Section IV presents all the three protocols [2] used in CryptoVerif language. In Sections V and VI, source code for CryptoVerif and the outputs of running those codes in CryptoVerif are discussed. Section VII introduces the proposed changes. Finally, Section VIII concludes the paper with suggestions for future work.

II. NOTATIONS AND PRIMITIVES

This section will briefly introduce the notations and primitives needed for implementation of CryptoVerif. In Tables I and II depict a list of symbols and notations used.

A. Notation:

Protocols are described using the dot (.) notation. For example, the encryption key *ek* of user U is denoted by *U.ek*. For two bit strings x, y, x||y denotes their concatenation, and x XOR y denotes their bitwise exclusive-OR. Finally, for any two entities, such as *U* and *S*, and a message m, *U* → *S* : *m* denotes that *U* sends *m* to *S*.

B. Cryptographic Primitives:

Three cryptographic primitives: Hash Function, Public Key Encryption, and Digital Signature are described in this section. They will be used in the protocols described in Section III. Detailed definition of the notations used can be found in [14]-[15].

1) Hash Function: A cryptographic hash function family is a set of hash functions HFs, such that each HF ϵ H is a mapping from {0, 1} m to {0, 1} n, where m, n ϵ N, and m > n. The security of a cryptographic hash function is defined in terms of an adversary's ability to invert the function (one-way property), and find collisions in the functions (collision-resistance property). Detailed security definitions are omitted from this paper. There are many forms of cryptographic hash functions. The National Institute of Standards and Technology (NIST) has recommendations for some of them [16]-[17].

2) Public Key Encryption: A public key encryption, E, involves Key Generation Algorithm (EKG), Encryption Algorithm (ENC), and Decryption Algorithm (DEC), with the associated security parameter 1λ and message space M, consists of the following three probabilistic polynomial-time primitives:

a) Key Generation: (ek, dk) ← EKG($1^λ$) Here, the input is the security parameter $1^λ$, and the output is pair of an encryption key ek and a decryption key dk.

TABLE I. GENERAL NOTATIONS AND SYMBOLS

Symbol	**Meaning**
SCADA	Supervisory Control and Data Acquisition
DNP3	Distributed Network Protocol Version 3
U_i	User Node (Smart meter) #i, i=1, 2, ...n
G	Central Gateway (Collector)
S	Supervisory Node (Substation)
Aux	Auxiliary time: Period of validity (T_1 & T_2)
CPU	Center Processing Unit
NIST	National Institute of Standard and Technology
XOR	Exclusive OR
LIST	List of all {U.ID, U.AID} Pairs
ε	Probability
f(ε)	Function of Probability

TABLE II. PROTOCOLS NOTATIONS & SYMBOLS

Symbol	**Meaning**
1^{λ}	Security Parameter
c	Ciphertext
U_i.ID	User Node Identity
ek	Public Key/Encryption Key
sk	Private Key or Signing Key
U_i.AID	User Node anonymous identity
$U_{i\text{-}pk}$	User Node public key
$U_{i\text{-}sk}$	User Node private key
G_i.ID	Central Gateway Identity
G_i.AID	Central Gateway anonymous identity
$G_{i\text{-}pk}$	Central Gateway public key
$G_{i\text{-}sk}$	Central Gateway private key
σ	Signature
s	Digital Signature Scheme
vk	Verification Key
$D_{SS.sk}$	Signing Key of s
$D_{SS.vk}$	Verification Key of s
$G_i.D_{SS.sk}$	Central Gatway signing key
$G_i.D_{SS.VK}$	Central Gateway verification key
U_i.r	User Node #i 's Reading, i=1, 2, …n
U_i.t	User Node #i 's Processor temperature, i=1, 2,
Hash(U_i.r)	Hash value for User Node #i 's reading, i=1, 2,
U_i.M	U_i.M = U_i.r XOR U_i.t
$S_{\text{-}pk}$	Supervisory public key
$S_{\text{-}sk}$	Supervisory private key
A-ID_i, A-ID_g , A-	Anonymous ID for Node, Central Gateway &
G_{cert}, $U_{i\text{-}cert}$, CR_i	Certificate of Central Gateway and User Node i
‖	Concatenation
E	Public Key Encryption
→	Send to
←	Result
DEC	Decryption Algorithm of E
dk	Decryption Key of E
EKG	Key Generation Algorithm of E
ENC	Encryption Algorithm of E
H	Cryptographic Hash Function Family
HF	Hash Function
M	Message Space
m	Message
SIG	Signature Algorithm of s
SKG	Key Generation Algorithm of s
VER	Verification Algorithm of s

b) ***Encryption:*** c ← ENC(ek,m) For this notation, the input is an encryption key ek ∈ EKG(1^{λ}) and a message m ∈ M, and the output is a ciphertext c.

c) ***Decryption*:** m ← DEC(dk, c) Here, the input is a decryption key dk and a ciphertext c, where (ek, dk) ∈ EKG (1^{λ}), m ∈ M, and c ∈ ENC(ek, m).

These need a correctness criterion, which is stated as follows: for every (ek, dk) ∈ EKG(1^{λ}), m ∈ M, and c ∈ ENC(ek, m), the probability that DEC(dk, c) ≠ m is negligible.

The security of the encryption scheme is defined in terms of an adversary's ability to learn partial information about the message underlying a ciphertext and is based on attack models, such as Chosen-Plaintext Attack and Chosen-Ciphertext Attack [18]. There are many forms of public key encryption algorithm. NIST has recommendations for factoring-based algorithms [19] and discrete logarithm-based algorithms [20].

3) Digital Signature Scheme: A digital signature scheme, S = (SKG, SIG, VER), with the associated security parameter 1^{λ} and message space M, consists of the following three probabilistic polynomial time algorithms:

a) Key Generation: (sk, vk) SKG(1^{λ}) For this notation, the input is security parameter 1^{λ} and the output is a pair of a signing key sk and a verification key vk.

b) Signature: σ ← SIG(sk,m) For this notation, the input is a signing key sk ∈ SKG(1^{λ}) and a message m ∈ M, and the output is a signature σ

c) Verification: 1/0 ← VER(vk, m, σ) For this notation, the input is a verification key vk, a message m, and a signature σ, where (sk, vk) ∈ SKG(1^{λ}), m ∈ M, and σ ∈ SIG(sk,m). The output is 1 for valid signature, and 0 for invalid signature. These need a correctness criterion, which is stated as follows: for every (sk, vk) ϵ SKG(1^{λ}), m ϵ M, and σ ϵ SIG(sk,m), the probability that VER(vk, m, σ) ≠ 1 is negligible.

The security of signature schemes is defined in terms of an adversary's ability to forge a signature and is based on attack models, such as Chosen-Message Attack. There are many forms of digital signature scheme. NIST has recommendations for some of them [21].

III. Overview of CryptoVerif

This section will present provable security and formal verification required for using the CryptoVerif tool. Also, this section will explain briefly the CryptoVerif code.

A. *Provable security and Formal verification*

When analyzing the security of cryptographic protocols, a notion of "provable security" is raised, where adversaries are modeled as probabilistic polynomial time Turing machines with capabilities and limitations of the verification tool. Through such modeling, one can prove that the cryptographic protocol is secure by showing that if there exists an adversary under the defined model that breaks the protocol, then the certain hard mathematical problem becomes easy to solve. A proof is then obtained via contradiction: since this problem is hard to solve, then it must be that the protocol is also hard to break. A security proof for a given protocol is a reduction from the protocol to a problem assumed to be hard. This reduction can be obtained via a sequence of games, where each game is a slight modification of the previous one.

Formal verifications, or formal methods, as defined in the Dolev-Yao et al [22] framework, is a method to obtain a proof. As shown in [23], the reductions of a proof are obtained via a "sequence of games" (also known as the game hopping technique), where each game differs from previous one by being slightly changed. The sequence of games is statistically or computationally indistinguishable from the point of view of an adversary. In such a proof, the initial game is the real attack game that models the adversary and the protocol. Then, two consecutive games will look either identical, or very close to each other in the view of the adversary.

1) Rename some variables. In this case the two games are perfectly identical.

2) Replace one variable x with another one y where the distributions are "statistically" indistinguishable. Here, the two Games are statistically identical except for negligible probabilities.

3) Replace one variable x with another one y where the distributions are "computational" indistinguishable - distinguishing two Games implies the ability of solving a certain computational hard problem.

The proof is obtained via a chain of reductions such that if an adversary is capable of breaking the initial game (given protocol) with certain probability ε, then he/she is also able to break the final game with probability function of $f(\varepsilon)$. Since the final game is assumed hard - in other words $f(\varepsilon)$ is negligible- it is implied that ε itself is also small.

In the final game, a certain known hard problem will be arrived at in which the adversary is believed to be incapable of solving.

B. *CryptoVerif*

CryptoVerif is an automatic tool to generate a sequence of games. CryptoVerif can also evaluate the probability of success of an attack against the protocol as a function of the probability of breaking each cryptographic primitive and of the number of sessions (exact security). A list of reserved words of the CryptoVerif tool syntax is listed in Table III:

1) Reading the output and games

As mentioned earlier, CryptoVerif presents the results in terms of a sequence of games. As one shall be seen in Section V, the sequence is presented as follows. Using the source code, CryptoVerif performs a compilation optimization to produce the initial game, game 0. This process does not change the content of the source code. In other words, the initial game is equivalent to the source code written in CryptoVerif syntax, as it performs a sequence of reductions through the chain of the games. Only slight difference is observed between each two consecutive games. Such differences may be due to one of the following reasons:

a) Removing an unused variable. This is done with simplification pass, see VI-C for instance.

b) Removing variables that do not have an impact on the game. This is done with findcond, see VI-B for instance.

c) Applying equivalence between certain cryptographic primitive and pre-defined probability; see VI-E for instance.

Through this sequence of the reductions, the final game, which is secured by assumption, is arrived at. This completes the overall proof. If an attacker is able to break the protocol which is equivalent to the initial Game, then the attacker will also be able to break the underlying encryption algorithm with probability of at least Penccoll, or break Game 7. These are illustrated in Section VI-G.

TABLE III. CRYPTOVERIF INSTRUCTIONS

Keyword	**Meaning**
const	declare a constant
expand	expand a cryptographic primitive
fun	abstract functions
if . . . then . . .	conditional flow control
in	input to a channel
out	output to a channel
let	assign value to a variable
new	declare a variable for a given type
proba	declare a probabilistic variable
process	main function
type	define a new type of variable

2) Limitations of CryptoVerif:

CryptoVerif is a tool to generate a chain of proofs in the form of a sequence of games, to show a reduction from a given protocol into a certain hard mathematical problem or assumed-hard problem. Such a proof does not guarantee the security of the final game. Thus, if an insecure hash function, for example SHA-1 [24] is used, CryptoVerif will still produce a valid reduction to SHA-1. However, the scheme will no longer be secure due to the insecurity of SHA-1. Another limitation of CryptoVerif is that it does not find redundancy in the protocols. The redundancy occurs when extra and maybe unnecessary cryptographic operations are performed. Such operations will not reduce the overall security of the system. Hence, from CryptoVerify point of view, those operations are not flagged as they are still technically correct.

IV. SMART METER SECURITY PROTOCOL

In this section, the three protocols [2] are presented. The protocols described in sections A and B are for the direct communication setting as shown in Figure 1, and the one described in section C is for the indirect communication setting as depicted in Figure 2. The direct and indirect communications are between the user node and the central gateway.

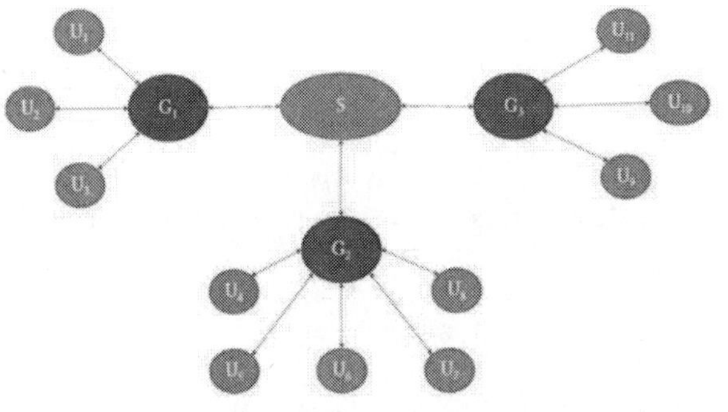

Figure 1. Direct communication.

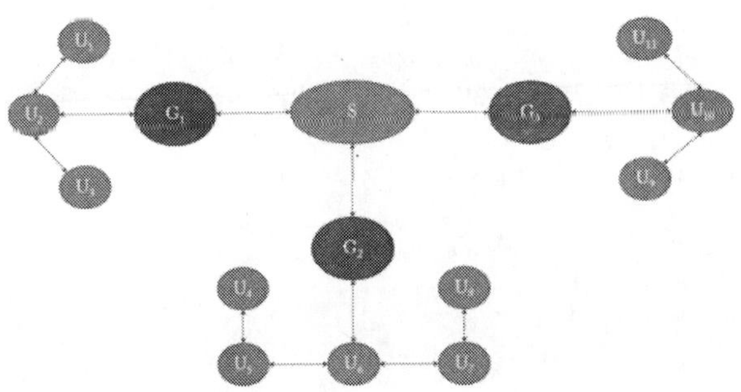

Figure 2. Indirect communication.

A. *Direct communication*

The first protocol consists of three processes: Enrollment and activation process, Security process, and Key update and exchange process.

1) Enrollment and Activation Process

In this process, the user nodes (smart meters) and the central gateways will be enrolled and activated so that they will be authenticated during the rest of the processes in sections IV-A-2 and IV-A-3. This process is as follows:

Step 1: The supervisory node S obtains the identities of all user nodes $\{U_i, ID\}_{i=1,2...}$ and identities and encryption keys of all central gateways $\{G_i.ID, G_i.ek\}_{i=1,2...}$

Step 2: S → $\{U_i\}_{i=1,2...}$: $\{G_i.ID, G_i.ek\}_{i=1,2...}$

S simply forwards to all user nodes the identities and encryption keys of all central gateways that it obtained in step 1.

Step 3: S → $\{G_i\}_{i=1,2...}$: $\{U_i.ID\}_{i=12...}$

S simply forwards the identities of all user nodes that were obtained in step 1 to all central gateways.

Step 4: G → U : $(m_3\sigma_3)$, where

m3 ← (U.ek || G.ID), and

σ_3 ← SIG(G.sk,m_3).

Here, G sends a request message and signature to U.

Step 5: U extracts G.ID from m_3 and validates it against the list obtained in step 1.

Step 6: If step 4 is successful, U → G : c_5 ← ENC(G.ek, m_5), where

m_5 ← (U.ID || U.ek).

Step 7: G decrypts c_5: m_5 ← DEC(G.dk, c5), extracts U.ID from m_5 and validates it against the list obtained in step 2. If validation is successful, G extracts U.ek from m5 and stores it.

2) Security Process

Once the nodes are activated, they will be able to send relevant data to the gateways during this process.

Step 1: U → G : c_1, where c_1 ← ENC(G.ek, m_1). Here, m_1 ← (U.r || U.t || U.m || h), U.r is U's reading, U.t is U's CPU temperature, and U.m ← (U.r XOR U.t). Finally, h ← HF(U.r).

Step 2: G decrypts c_1 : m_1 ← DEC(G.dk, c_1), extracts (U.ID, U.t, U.m, h) from m_1, computes U.r ← (U.t XOR U.m), and checks if h = HF(U.r). If the check is successful, G stores U.r.

3) Key update and exchange process

The last process of protocol A is a process for both nodes and gateways to update their keys. The process of the gateways will be shown as follows in the steps below. The process to update keys for U is similar, and therefore omitted for simplicity.

Step 1: G → U : (c_1 || G.ID), where

c_1 ← ENC(U.ek, G.ek || G.vk || σ), and

σ ← SIG(G.sk, G.ek || G.vk).

Step 2: U decrypts c_1: m1 ← DEC(U.dk, c_1), extracts (G.ek, G.vk, σ) from m_1, and checks if VER(G.vk, G.ek || G.vk, σ) = 1. If the check is successful, U stores G.ek and G.vk.

B. *Direct communication- Certificates*

The second protocol consists of three processes: Enrollment and activation process, Security process, and

Key update and exchange process. Compared to protocol A, here the major difference will be the presence of certificates.

1) Enrollment and activation process

The purpose of this process is to establish enrollments for nodes and gateways with the help of certificates. Some of the variables used below will be used in other sections preserving the same meaning.

Step1: $G \rightarrow S : c1 \leftarrow ENC(S.ek, m1)$, where
$m_1 \leftarrow (G.AID \,||\, G.ID \,||\, G.ek)$
Step2: $S \rightarrow G : c_2 \leftarrow ENC(S.ek, cert_2)$, where
$cert_2 \leftarrow (m_2 \,||\, \sigma_2)$
$\sigma_2 \leftarrow SIG(S.sk, m_2)$
$m_2 \leftarrow (m_1 \,||\, AUX)$.
$m_1 \leftarrow DEC(S.dk, c_1)$.
Step3: $U \rightarrow S : c_3 \leftarrow ENC(S.ek, m_3)$, where
$m_3 \leftarrow (U.AID \,||\, U.ID \,||\, U.ek)$.
Step4: $S \rightarrow U : c_4 \leftarrow ENC(S.ek, cert_4)$, where
$cert_4 \leftarrow (m_4 \,||\, \sigma_4)$
$\sigma_4 \leftarrow SIG(S.sk, m_4)$.
$m_4 \leftarrow (m_3 \,||\, AUX)$.
$m_3 \leftarrow DEC(S.dk, c_3)$.
Step5: $S \rightarrow G$: LIST, where
LIST is a list of all {U.ID, U.AID} pairs.

2) Security Process

Once connections are established, this process, is adopted to exchange data between user nodes and central gateways.

Step1: U and G exchange their certificates.
Step2: Each party verifies the certificate to obtain the other party's ek and ID.
Step3: sk and ID are accepted if AUX information is also verified.
Step4: Apply the steps of A-2.

3) Certificate Update Process

This last process of protocol B allows the users and gateways to update their certificates.

Step1: S informs U and G to create new keys
Step2: Both parties will follow same steps as B-1 to get new certificates.

C. Indirect Communication

The last protocol consists of three processes: Enrollment, Activation and Certificate Exchange, Secure Reading Collection Process, and Key Update and Certificate Exchange Process.

1) Enrollment, Activation, and Certificate Exchange

This process allows user nodes and central gateways to exchange their certifications.

Step1: $Ui \rightarrow G : c_1 \leftarrow ENC(G.ek, m_1)$, where
$m_1 \leftarrow (U_i.AID \,||\, U_i.ID)$
Step2: $G \rightarrow U_i : e_2 \leftarrow ENC(U_i.ek, m_2 \,||\, \sigma_2)$, where
$\sigma_2 \leftarrow SIG(G.sk, m_2)$
$m_2 \leftarrow U_i.E.pk \,||\, U_i.AID \,||\, U_i.AUX$
Step3: On node U_j for $i \neq j$: forward the message.
Step4: On node U_i:
$m_2 \,||\, \sigma_2 \leftarrow DEC(U_i.sk, e_2)$;
U_i Store m_2 and σ_2 as the message and certificate pair.

2) Secure Reading Collection Process

This process allows user nodes to send their readings to a central gateway, via either a direct connection or an indirect connection. The data flow is omitted due to the involvement of multiple entities.

Step1: Processing at node U_i:
$U_i.T \leftarrow TRNG$;
$U_i.R \leftarrow$ reading of the data;
$U_i.M \leftarrow U_i.T$ XOR $U_i.R$;
$m1 \leftarrow U_i.M \,||\, Hash(U_i.R) \,||\, U_i.T$
$\sigma_1 \leftarrow SIG(U_i.sk, m_1)$
$U_i.Y \leftarrow ENC(G.ek, m_1 \,||\, \sigma_1)$
Step2: $U_i \rightarrow U_{i-1}: c_2$, where
$c_2 \leftarrow ENC(U_{i-1}.ek, U_i.Y)$
Step3: On node U_{i-1}:
Compute $U_{i-1}.Y$ as in step 1;
$U_i.Y \leftarrow DEC(U_{i-1}.dk, c_2)$
Step4: $U_{i-1} \rightarrow U_{i-2} : c_4$, where
Using a pseudonym number generation to randomize the output (c_4)
$b \leftarrow$ a random bit;
if $b = 1$, $c_4 \leftarrow ENC(U_{i-2}.ek, U_i.Y \,||\, U_{i-1}.Y)$
else $c_4 \leftarrow ENC(U_{i-2}.ek, U_{i-1}.Y \,||\, U_i.Y)$
Step5: Repeat steps 1-4 for all other user nodes until G is reached.
Step6: Processing at G:
$m_j \leftarrow DEC(G.dk, c_j)$; where $j = 1$ to N
Extract $U_i.Y$ from m_j for each user;
$m_1 \,||\, \sigma_1 \leftarrow DEC(G.dk, U_i.Y)$;
Step7: Check the correctness of σ_1
Extract $U_i.T$, $U_i.M$ and recover $U_i.R$
G Store the reading $U_i.R$ if σ_1 is verified

3) Key Update and Certificate Exchange Process

This last process allows the entities to update their keys and the certificates associated with them.

Step1: $G \rightarrow U : e_1 \,||\, G.ID$, where
$(G.ek', G.dk') \leftarrow KG(1^{\lambda})$
$(G.sk', G.vk') \leftarrow KG(1^{\lambda})$
$e_1 \leftarrow ENC(U.ek, m_1 \,||\, \sigma_1)$
$m_1 \leftarrow G.ek' \,||\, G.sk'$
$\sigma_1 \leftarrow SIG(G.sk, m_1)$
Step2: On node U
$m_1 \,||\, \sigma_1 \leftarrow DEC(U.dk, e_1)$
Extract $G.ek'$ and $G.vk'$ from m_1
If $VER(G.vk, m_1, \sigma_1) = 1$, accept $G.ek'$ and $G.vk'$
Step3: $U \rightarrow G : e_3 \,||\, U.AID$, where
$(U.ek', U.dk') \leftarrow KG(1^{\lambda})$
$(U.sk', U.vk') \leftarrow KG(1^{\lambda})$
$m_3 \leftarrow U.ek' \,||\, U.sk'$
$\sigma_3 \leftarrow SIG(U.sk, m_3)$
$e_3 \leftarrow ENC(G.ek, m_3 \,||\, \sigma_3)$
Step4: On node G

$m_3 \| \sigma_3 \leftarrow$ DEC(G.dk, e_3)
Extract U.ek` and U.vk` from m_3
If VER(U.vk, m_3, σ_3) = 1, accept U.ek` and U.vk`

V. CRPTOVERIF CODE

The CryptoVerif code for process A-1 of protocol A (section IV-A-1) will be provided in this section. All the code sections share the same set of pre-defined parameters and macros. The sections display all the related symbols, notations, functions, and algorithms for all the related entities, namely Nodes, Gateways, and Servers, are defined using CryptoVerif language as follows:

A. Defining hosts, nodes, gateways and server

```
t y p e host [ bounded ] .
c o n s t Node : host . (* node s)
c o n s t Gateway : host . (* gateway)
c o n s t Server : host . (* server)
```

B. Defining Parameters

The relevant macros are given as below. The spaces are the locations where the variables, such as the reading R or the time T, are drawn from.

```
t y p e Rspace [ bounded ] .
t y p e AIDspace [ bounded ] .
t y p e AUXspace [ bounded ] .
```

C. hash function

The hash functions, encryption functions, and decryption functions are defined. A hash function has two inputs, an input channel hc1 and an output channel hc2. The exact hash function to be used (such as SHA-2) is not defined here since only abstract functionality is required here.

```
param qH [ noninteractive ] .
channel hc1 , hc2 .
let hash oracle = ! qH i n ( hc1 , x : bit string ) ;
out ( hc2 , hash ( hk , x ) ) .
```

D. Public key encryption parameters

Public key, secret key (private key), seed, block size, and key generation parameters are defined below.

```
t y p e pkey [ bounded ] .
t y p e blocksize [ fixed ] .

proba Penc .
proba Penccoll .
expand IND CCA2 public key enc ( keyseed, pkey, skey, blocksize, bit string, seed, skgen, pkgen, enc, dec, injbot, Z, Penc, Penccoll).
```

E. Digital signature algorithms

The key locations, ciphertext spaces, and the seeds for both key generations and encryptions are defined. Then, the probability of an adversary breaking the scheme is also defined in order to achieve a meaningful reduction at the end. The encryption algorithm will be equivalent to an expansion over the above variables. The codes for signature function are as follows:

```
t y p e sskey [ bounded ] .
proba Psign .
proba Psigncoll .
expand UF CMA signature (keyseed, spkey, sskey, sblocksize, signature, sseed, sskgen, spkgen, sign, check, Psign, Psigncoll).
```

F. Defining I/O channels

The key spaces and ciphertext spaces are defined, as well as the seeds for both key generations and signatures. Also, as in encryption scheme, the probability of an adversary breaking the scheme is also defined, in order to achieve a meaningful reduction in the end. The signature algorithm is then an expansion over the above variables. In CryptoVerif, the variables of different types are not compatible. To solve this issue, conversion functions to resolve the incompatibility between different types are defined. To save space the conversion functions are omitted. The last step before protocol simulation is to define the input and output channels. Depending on the actual protocol, the number of channels may vary as defined below:

```
c h a n n e l c0 , c1 , c2 , c3 , c4 , c5 , start , finish .
```

G. Defining Gateway parameters

```
new gid : IDspace ;
new gateway seed : keyseed ;
l e t gspk = spkgen ( gateway signseed ) i n
l e t gssk = sskgen ( gateway signseed ) i n
```

H. Defining server (substation) parameters

```
new sid : IDspace ;
new serverseed : keyseed ;
l e t sspk = spkgen ( server signseed ) i n
l e t sssk = sskgen ( serversignseed ) i n
```

I. Defining user node (smart meter) parameters

```
new nid : IDspace ;
new nodeseed : keyseed ;
l e t nepk = pkgen ( nodeseed ) i n
l e t nesk = skgen ( nodeseed ) i n
```

J. Message generation and signature

The gateway generates a message which is the concatenation of Node's encryption key and Gateway's ID. The Gateway also signs this message.

```
l e t process step 4 =
i n ( c0 , (= nepk ,= gid ,= gssk , hostX : host ) ) ;
i f ( hos tX = Gateway ) t h e n
o u t ( c1 , (m, sigma ) ) .
```

K. Extracting the gateway's ID

The node extracts the Gateway's ID from the message and validates it against the list obtained in G above. It then forms another message by concatenating the ID with the Node's public key. If the code in J above is successful, the message will be encrypted with the public key of the central gateway.

```
let process step 5 6 =
in ( c1 , (msg : sblocksiz e , gidrec : IDspace , =
nid , =nepk , =gepk , hostX : host ) ) ;
if ( hostX = Node ) t h e n
new encseed : seed ;
let cipher = enc (m2 , gepk , encseed ) in
out ( c2 , cipher ) .
```

L. Message decryption

The Gateway decrypts the message and extracts the Node's ID.

```
let process step 7 =
in (c3, (= gesk, cipher: bitstring,=nepk,=nid,hostX: host));
if ( nidrec = nid ) t h e n
out ( c4 , ( nid , nepk ) ) .
```

M. Assembling all process

Finally, a master process is called to assemble all those processes

```
p r o c e s s
i n ( start , ( ) ) ;
o u t ( finish , ( nid , nepk , gid , gs sk , ge sk ) ) ;
( process step 4 | process step 5 6 | process step 7 )
```

VI. CRYPTOVERIF RESULTS

To begin with, a block diagram of the reduction flow is presented in Figure 3. Then, the details of the proofs are illustrated for section IV-A-1 as follows:

A. Game 1 - Initial State

```
in ( s t a r t , ( ) ) ;
new gid 218 : IDspa c e ;
new gateway seed : keyseed ;
let gepk : pkey = pkgen ( gateway seed ) in
let gesk : skey = skgen ( gateway seed ) in
new serversignseed : skeyseed ;
let sspk : spkey = spkgen ( serversignseed ) in
let sssk : sskey = sskgen ( serversignseed ) in
new nid : IDspace ;
new nodeseed : keyseed ;
if ( hostX 220 = Gateway ) t h e n
new sigseed : sseed ; 23
let m: sblocksize = concat 5 ( gid 218 , nepk 219 ) i n
let sigma : signature = sign (m, gssk , sigseed ) in
out ( c1 , (m, sigma ) )) j (
in ( c1 , (msg : sblocksize , gidrec : IDspace , =
nid , =nepk 219 , =gepk , hostX 221 : host ) );
if ( hostX 221 = Node ) t h e n
let concat 5 ( gid 223 : IDspace , nepk 222 : pkey ) = msg in
if ( gid 223 = gidrec ) t h e n
let m2 : blocksize = concat 4 ( nid , nepk 222 ) in
new encseed : seed ;
let cipher 2 2 4 : bitstring = enc (m2 , gepk ,encseed ) i n
out ( c2 , cipher 2 2 4 ) ) j (
in ( c3 , (= gesk , cipher 2 2 6 : bitstring , =
nepk 219 , =nid , hostX 225 : host ) ) ;
if ( nidrec = nid ) t h e n
out ( c4 , ( nid , nepk 219 ) )
```

B. Difference between Game 1 and 2

In game 2, the find condition function, findcond, is applied to remove the assignments for the following variables in the code: gspk, sepk,sesk, sspk,sssl and nesk. These are the variables that were not used in the game but necessary during the execution. For example, the public key for the central gateway gspk was not used, but since its secret key is crucial to the proof, it is still necessary to generate this key for the protocol. To sum up, this modification yields the removal of the following lines of code:

```
l e t gspk : spkey = spkgen ( gateway signseed ) in
new sid : IDspace ;
l e t sssk : sskey = sskgen ( serversignseed) in
l e t nesk : skey = skgen ( nodeseed ) in
```

C. Difference between Game 2 and 3

In Game 3, a simplification process is performed to remove the following lines:

```
new sid : IDspace ;
new serverseed : keyseed ;
new serversignseed : skeyseed ;
```

D. Difference between Game 3 and 4

In Game 4, the tool tries to remove assignments for the variable nepk. This yields:

```
- out ( f i n i s h , ( nid , nepk 241 , gid 240 , gssk ,
gesk ) ) ;
+ out ( finish , ( nid , pkgen ( nodeseed ) , gid 240 ,
gssk , gesk ) ) ;
in ( c0 , (= nepk 241 , =gid 240 , = gssk ) ) ;
+ in ( c0 , (= pkgen ( nodeseed ) , =gid 240 , = gssk ) );
l e t m: sblocksize = concat 5 ( gid 240 ,
nepk 241 ) i n
+ l e t m: sblocksize = concat 5 ( gid 240 , pkgen (
nodeseed ) ) in
in ( c3 , (= gesk , cipher 2 4 5 : bitstring , =
nepk 241 , = nid ) ) ;
+ in ( c3 , (= gesk , cipher 2 4 5 : bitstring , =pkgen
( nodeseed ) , = nid ) ) ;
out ( c4 , ( nid , nepk 241 ) )
+ out ( c4 , ( nid , pkgen ( nodeseed ) ) )
```

E. Difference between Game 4 and 5

The formal reductions are performed in Game 5, where the tool applies the following:

IND CCA2(enc) with node seed, encseed = probability Penccoll + Penc(time(context for Game 4) + time, 0). This equation indicates the security of the underlying encryption primitive, depending on the ciphertext indistinguishability against chosen ciphertext attacks (IND-CCA), which is a function of the probability of finding collisions (Penccoll) and the time of encryption (Penc). With a few substitutions for some of the variables, this yields:

```
- new nodeseed : keyseed ;
- out ( finish , ( nid , pkgen ( nodeseed ) , gid 240 ,
- new encseed : seed ; 11
- l e t cipher 2 4 4 : bitstring = enc (m2 , gepk ,
encseed ) in
+ l e t @8 x 285 : blocksize = m2 i n
+ l e t @8 y 284 : pkey = gepk i n
+ l e t cipher 2 4 4 : bitstring = enc (@8 x 285 ,
@8 y 284 , @8 r3 287 ) in
```

F. Difference between Game 5 and 6

During this step, the individual variables for public keys and ciphertexts are removed. Their values are saved. These variables are passed directly to the encryption function for compactness.

```
- l e t @8 x 285 : blocksize = m2 in
- l e t @8 y 284 : pkey = gepk in
- l e t cipher 2 4 4 : bitstrin g = enc (@8 x 285 ,
@8 y 284 , @8 r3 287 ) in
+ l e t cipher 2 4 4 : bitstring = enc (m2,gepk,@8 r3 287 ) in
```

G. Difference between Game 6 and 7

Since the encryption function in previous step has been made explicit without referring to

run-time variables, there is no need to use an encryption seed anymore. This is reflected in this code below:

```
new encseed 286 : seed ;
```

Once Game 7 is reached, a conclusion is generated via the following inequality:

ADV(Game1; Initial Game) $\leq$ Penccoll + Penc(time(Game 4) + time, 0) + ADV(Game7; Initial Game)   (1)

This implies that the Advantage an adversary gains to be able to break the initial Game is less than or equal the sum of three quantities; the probability to break the encryption scheme Penccoll, the time to perform various polynomial time algorithms such as key generation and encryption Penc(time(Game 4) + time, 0), and the Advantage of breaking the last Game by the adversary ADV(Game7; Initia Game). By assumption, this last quantity is bounded by:

ADV(Game7; Initial Game) $\leq$ 0   (2)

The last two quantities are both small. Hence, if the adversary is able to break the IV-A-1 process, Penccoll must be non-negligible, which implies that the adversary must also be able to break the underlying encryption algorithm.

H. Summary of Statistical Analysis

The summery of the statistical analysis for the three protocols and the number of Games that is required to obtain a proof is presented in table IV. The following equations are used in the statistical analysis

Pre-compile optimization = 1 – (No. of lines in the initial Game/No. of lines of codes)   (3)

Total run time optimization = 1 – (No. of lines in the final game/No. of lines in the initial Game)   (4)

Average run time optimization = Total run time optimization/Number of Games   (5)

Total improvement = 1 – (No. of lines in the final Game/No. of lines of codes)   (6)

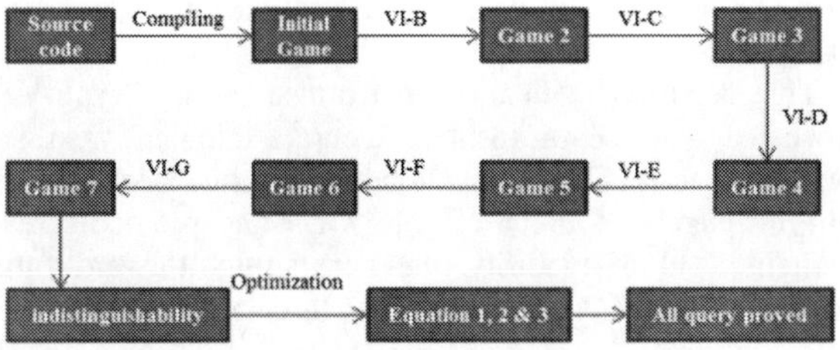

Figure 3. Reduction flow for A-1.

TABLE IV. GAMES SATATISTICS FOR THE PROTOCOLS

	Section								
Variables	A-1	A-2	A-3	B-1	B-2	B-3	C-1	C-2	C-3
Number of Games	8	3	11	7	3	7	3	3	17
Line of codes	177	243	185	186	247	196	182	258	238
Line in the Initial Game	40	49	39	50	50	50	49	60	66
Line in the Final Game	30	40	32	46	40	46	46	56	60
Pre-Coupile Optimization (Eq.3) %	77.4	79.8	78.9	73.1	79.7	74.5	73.1	76.7	72.3
Run time optimization (total) (Eq. 4) %	25	18.4	17.9	8.0	20	8.0	6.1	6.7	9.1
Average run time optimization (Eq.5) %	3.13	6.13	1.63	1.14	6.67	1.14	2.04	2.23	0.53
Total improvement (Eq. 6) %	83.1	83.5	82.7	75.3	83.8	76.5	74.7	78.3	74.8

VII. PROPOSED CHANGES AND IMPROVEMENTS

In addition to the automated analysis from CryptoVerif, a preliminary manual analysis was also performed and the following findings are observed. First, protocol A does not state how authenticity was established. It was assumed that entities involved in this protocol obtain certain mutual authenticity through some channel not specified by the protocol. Inappropriate authentication methods may lead to potential attacks. Nonetheless, it is common that in practice one may rely on pre-established authenticity. It is also worth noting that in protocol B and C, certificates are used for authentication. Second, some of the operations seem to be redundant.

For example, in protocols A and B, signatures are encrypted before they are sent. Thus, this operation does not add any additional security features to the protocol. Third, in protocol C, the forward message employs a random bit to determine the sequence of concatenating the encrypted readings Y_{i-1} and Y_i. This design is adhoc and a security proof for this is not straightforward. Nonetheless, it is noted that this operation at least will not reduce the overall security.

VIII. CONCLUSION AND FUTURE WORK

In this paper, a formal analysis of three security protocols for the communication of smart meters was performed using CryptoVerif. A proof is produced through the reduction of a sequence of games. The analysis showed that the three schemes have no flaws in their security. In addition, a manual analysis of the protocol was performed and some redundancy was observed. This redundancy does not impact the overall security of the protocol, but it is highly likely that the protocol will be more efficient once the redundancy is removed.

The security evaluation performed with CryptoVerif revealed that the protocol is secure. A logical next step would be to perform simulation and benchmarking to judge the efficiency of the protocols. Once the protocols reach certain level of maturity, the next straightforward future work will be the deployment of the three protocols.

REFERENCES

[1] Draft Smart Grid Cyber Security Strategy and Requirements, NIST IR 7628, Sept, 2009

[2] M. Saed, K. Daimi, and N. Al-Holou, "Approaches for Securing Smart Meters in Smart Grid Networks," International Journal On Advances in Systems and Measurements, pp. 265–274, 2017.

[3] M. Majdalawieh, F. Parisi-Presicce, and D. Wijesekera, DNPSec: Distributed Network Protocol Version 3 (DNP3) Security Framework. Dordrecht: Springer Netherlands, 2006, pp. 227–234. [Online]. Available: https://doi.org/10.1007/1-4020-5261-8 36, [retrieved: May, 2018].

[4] TriangleMicroWorks, "Modbus and DNP3 Communication Protocols,"2017.[Online].Available: https://scadahacker.com/library/Documents/ICSProtocols/TriangleMicroworks-Modbus-DNP3Comparison.pdf, [retrieved: May, 2018].

[5] B. Blanchet, "CryptoVerif: Cryptographic Protocol Verifier in the Computational Model," INRIA, Tech. Rep., 2017. [Online]. Available: http://prosecco.gforge.inria.fr/personal/bblanche/cryptoverif/, [retrieved: May, 2018].

[6] K. Bhargavan, B. Blanchet, and N. Kobeissi, "Verified models and reference implementations for the TLS 1.3 standard candidate," in 2017 IEEE Symposium on Security and Privacy, SP 2017, San Jose, CA, USA, May 22-26, 2017, 2017, pp. 483– 502. [Online]. Available: https://doi.org/10.1109/SP.2017.26, [retrieved: May, 2018].

[7] T. Dierks and E. Rescorla, The Transport Layer Security (TLS) Protocol Version 1.2. Internet Engineering Task Force, 2008. [Online]. Available: https://tools.ietf.org/html/rfc5246, [retrieved: May, 2018].

[8] B. Dowling, M. Fischlin, F. Gnther, and D. Stebila, "A cryptographic analysis of the tls 1.3 handshake protocol candidates," Cryptology ePrint Archive, Report 2015/914, 2015, https://eprint.iacr.org/2015/914, [retrieved: May, 2018].

[9] X. Li, J. Xu, Z. Zhang, D. Feng, and H. Hu, "Multiple handshakes security of tls 1.3 candidates," in 2016 IEEE Symposium on Security and Privacy (SP), May 2016, pp. 486–505.

[10] C. J. F. Cremers, M. Horvat, J. Hoyland, S. Scott, and T. van der Merwe, "A comprehensive symbolic analysis of tls 1.3," in CCS, 2017, pp. 1773-1788.

[11] B. Blanchet and D. Pointcheval, "Automated security proofs with sequences of games," in CRYPTO'06, ser. Lecture Notes in Computer Science, C. Dwork, Ed., vol. 4117. Santa Barbara, CA: Springer, Aug. 2006, pp. 537–554.

[12] M. Bellare and P. Rogaway, "The exact security of digital signatures-how to sign with rsa and rabin," in Advances in Cryptology — EUROCRYPT '96, U. Maurer, Ed. Berlin, Heidelberg: Springer Berlin Heidelberg, 1996, pp. 399–416.

[13] R. L. Rivest, A. Shamir, and L. M. Adleman, "A method for obtaining digital signatures and public-key cryptosystems," Commun. ACM, vol. 21, no. 2, pp. 120–126, 1978.

[14] B. Blanchet, "Automatic verification of security protocols in the symbolic model: the verifier ProVerif," in Foundations of Security Analysis and Design VII, FOSAD Tutorial Lectures, ser. Lecture Notes in Computer Science, A. Aldini, J. Lopez, and F. Martinelli, Eds. Springer, 2014, vol. 8604, pp. 54–87.

[15] J. Katz and Y. Lindell, Introduction to Modern Cryptography, Second Edition, 2nd ed. Chapman & Hall/CRC, 2014.

[16] S. Goldwasser and M. Bellare, "Lecture Notes on Cryptography," MIT, Tech. Rep., 2008. [Online]. Available: https://cseweb.ucsd.edu/_mihir/papers/gb.pdf, [retrieved: May, 2018].

[17] Q. H. Dang, Secure Hash Standard (SHS). National Institute of Standards and Technology, 2015. [Online]. Available: https://dx.doi.org/10.6028/NIST.FIPS.180-4, [retrieved: May, 2018].

[18] NIST, SHA-3 Standard: Permutation-Based Hash and Extendable-Output Functions. National Institute of Standards and Technology, 2015. [Online]. Available: http://doi.org/10.6028/NIST.FIPS.202, [retrieved: May, 2018].

[19] M. Bellare, A. Desai, D. Pointcheval, and P. Rogaway, "Relations among notions of security for public-key encryption schemes," in CRYPTO, 1998, pp. 26–45.

[20] E. Barker, L. Chen, and D. Moody, Recommendation for Pair-Wise Key-Establishment Schemes Using Integer Factorization Cryptography. National Institute of Standards and Technology, 2014. [Online]. Available: http://doi.org/10.6028/NIST.SP.800-56Br1, [retrieved: May, 2018].

[21] E. Barker, L. Chen, A. Roginsky, and M. Smid, "Recommendation for Pair-Wise Key Establishment Schemes Using Discrete Logarithm Cryptography," National Institute of Standards and Technology, 2013. [Online]. Available: http://doi.org/10.6028/NIST.SP.800-56Ar2, [retrieved: May, 2018].

[22] E. Barker, "Digital Signature Standard (DSS)," National Institute of Standards and Technology, 2013. [Online]. Available: http://doi.org/10.6028/NIST.FIPS.186-4, [retrieved: May, 2018].

[23] D. Dolev and A. C. Yao, "On the security of public key protocols," IEEE Trans. Information Theory, vol. 29, no. 2, pp. 198–207, 1983. [Online]. Available: https://doi.org/10.1109/TIT.1983.1056650, [retrieved: May, 2018].

[24] M. Bellare and P. Rogaway, "The security of triple encryption and a framework for code-based game-playing proofs," in Advances in Cryptology - EUROCRYPT 2006, S. Vaudenay, Ed. Berlin, Heidelberg: Springer Berlin Heidelberg, 2006, pp. 409–426.

[25] X. Wang, Y. L. Yin, and H. Yu, "Finding collisions in the full SHA-1," in Advances in Cryptology - CRYPTO 2005: 25th Annual International Cryptology Conference, Santa Barbara, California, USA, August 14-18, 2005, Proceedings, 2005, pp. 17–36. [Online]. Available: https://doi.org/10.1007/11535218 2, [retrieved: May, 2018].

AMBLoRa: a Wireless Tracking and Sensor System Using Long Range Communication to Monitor Animal Behavior

Thierry Antoine-Santoni
antoine-santoni@univ-corse.fr
UMR CNRS 6134 SPE
University of Corsica
Corte, France

Jean-Sebastien Gualtieri
js.gualtieri@sitec.corsica
SITEC
Parc Technologique
d'Erbajolo
BP 651 20601 Furiani

François-Marie Manicacci
manicacci_fm@univ-corse.fr
UMR CNRS 6134 SPE
University of Corsica
Corte, France

Antoine Aiello
aiello@univ-corse.fr
UMS CNRS 3114 Stella Mare
University of Corsica
Biguglia, France

***Abstract*—The University of Corsica decided to create in 2010 the platform STELLA MARE (Sustainable TEchnologies for LittoraL Aquaculture and MArine Research) and its platform CNRS-Università di Corsica leads a project called AMB.I.EN.T.E (AMBient Intelligence for Environment using Technical Efficiency) to develop some tools to follow the terrestrial and underwater activities of animal. Global Positioning System (GPS) is considered as an essential key in the monitoring of animal activity. Indeed, the knowledge of the movement, the reproduction and spawning areas are important for the researchers. We were able to study some research on GPS tracking system however the energy consumption, a quick deployment and real-time data visualization are not clearly expressed in a same technical solution. In this paper, we introduce a prototype of GPS tracker system using LoRa (for Long Range) technology according to these three previous needs.**

Keywords: GPS; LoRa; Tracking System; IoT

I. INTRODUCTION

The continuous tracking devices can be fine in several applications in the literature. Indeed, in several experiments (patients, vehicles, objects, etc.), the researchers try to optimize the devices to allow a complete monitoring and long life time of the system. Monitoring animal behavior is an important research topic to understand the relations between the animals and their environment. To know the position of the animal, we can distinguish two types of action:

- Active tracking where the animal is equipped by a tag (sonar, RFID, etc.) and the researcher try to detect, to find a signal in a determined area
- Passive tracking where the signal is send towards the research.

The second method is often based on Global Positioning System inserted in a collar.

In [1], the authors have collected more information about GSP tracking works in Australia to explain the relative success of GPS Collars. Indeed, it appears a clear benefit of these solutions however the main used tools are not consumption optimized, real-time configured and long range developed. The two mains solutions [2] [3] cited in this study demonstrate clearly their benefits but we note some lack in our research approach : a real time data visualization, a long life battery and wireless network system manageable. The University of Corsica leads a project called AMB.I.EN.T.E (AMBient Intelligence for Environment using Technical Efficiency) to develop some tools to follow the terrestrial and underwater activities of animals ; it was financed by an European Regional Development Fund (ERDF) and the Regional council of Corsica.

In [2], the authors try to evaluate the state of art in the using of LoRa based technologies. The first conclusions of this contribution show the capacity of long range communication and low power consumption of this technology in this area of research. Numbers of application [3]-[6] use this LoRa technology showing the potential of this communication media in the tracking system.

We propose in Section II a survey of animal monitoring tool in this research area. We introduce in Section III the AMBLoRa system and we present in Section IV the main results. We conclude in Section V with the future evolution of our system.

II. A SURVEY IN THIS AREA OF RESEARCH

In this section, we propose to discuss on different major works on wildlife monitoring system using a collar approach.

LynxNet is a wild animal monitoring system using sensor network [9] with an animal-centric paradigm. This system is based on Tmote Mini sensor, with a 433 MHz transceiver, is mobile sensing and uses sparse radio connectivity network. The LinxNet collar device produces two types of data:

1. GPS location with temperature, humidity and ambient light,
2. 3D accelometer and 2D gyroscope to calculate motion vector.

This LynxNet prototype is interesting but we do not have precisions on the components consumption and battery life time.

ZebraNet [10] uses a wireless system to monitor the Zebra migration in Kenya. Based on energy consumption approach, the authors try to conciliate accuracy and energy efficiency. An important step in their research and development activities is to use two separate microcontrollers, one for the sensors software and another for GPS, to reduce energy budget. We can note the incapacity to communicate on more than one kilometer.

The wildCENSE illustrated is considered by the authors [11] as a new approach of wildlife monitoring based on a wireless sensor system different of ZebraNet. It is a WSN system to monitor the behavior and migration patterns of Swam Deer. Based on GPS and different sensors (temperature, humidity, accelerometer and light), the wildCENSE node manages the energy consumption by active or sleeping states. The data are collected every 3 minutes and a data transmission towards the base station is allowed every 30 minutes. The system proposes a range of more than a kilometer.

In [12], the authors introduce a system using Long-Range Wireless Sensor Network for Geo-location for livestock animals tracking. The system illustrated shows the capacity of dynamic tracking and LoRa capacity however there is no approach on energy consumption and real-time. A Wildlife Monitoring System [12] was developed using a special IoT Infrastructure. Based on a hybrid communication system, using LoRaWan standard and Bluetooth Low Energy (BLE), WMS. The capacity to communicate with a low power consumption on several kilometers is an important point in this system.

WMS simulation results seem clearly an efficient architecture using two kinds of communication support however the information of battery life and the real-time monitoring system are not presented.

The collar approach and Lora technology are clearly important benefit points. However we can note some needs in our vision on the new design of wildlife tracking system comparison as showed on Table 1.

TABLE I. COMPARISON OF COLLAR SYSTEM FOR ANIMAL TRACKING

Important Contributions	**Energy**	**RT Data**	**Long range**	**quick deployment**
LynxNet[9]	+	+	-	-
ZebraNet [10]	-	-	+	-
Wildcense [11]			+	+
WMS [12]	-	-	++	-

After this survey of major works on animal tracking system using a collar, we decided to develop our collar according to four needs for our experiment : quickly deployable, energy efficient with relative real-time data visualization system associated. We propose in previous part a presentation of our solution and the first results in this work.

III. AMBLoRa : GPS TRACKING SYSTEM AND RELATIVE REAL-TIME DATA VISUALIZATION

We describe in this part the method implemented for the GPS tracking of Corsican deer (*Cervus elaphus corsicanus*) [13]. We made a tracking collar consisting of a waterproof case containing the AMBLoRa card integrated in a Lora system architecture.

The monitoring experiment described took place on the east coast of Corsica Island (red point on Figure 1) in an enclosure of the regional natural park of Corsica [14].

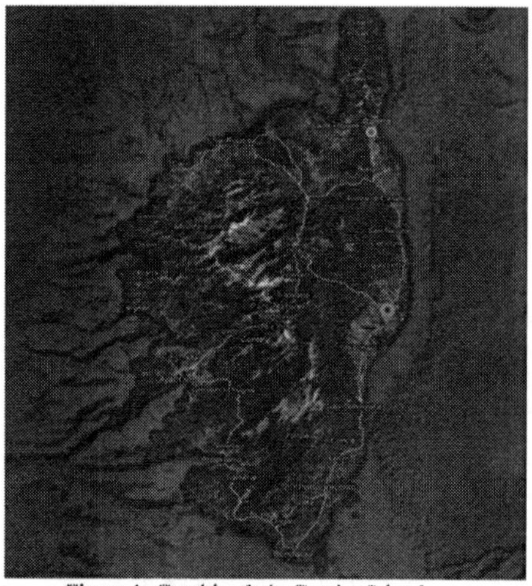

Figure 1: Casabianda in Corsica Island

Deers coming from Sardinia, pass by an enclosure before being released in Corsica. This is the case for the Casabianda enclosure (Figure 2). This enclosure of approximately 20.5 ha is used to keep the deer in semi-freedom and to prevent any health risks. The plant tissue is mainly composed of small bushes and some trees. The ground is relatively flat. There is no electrical source on site but GSM coverage in the area is good for our operators. About 40 individuals were identified in the enclosure in 2015. We can see in this Casabianda closed space (Figure 7 red lines) the area where the staff feed the deers (yellow circle) and clearing areas (green circles). After a time of quarantine, they are released in the Corsican Mountains.

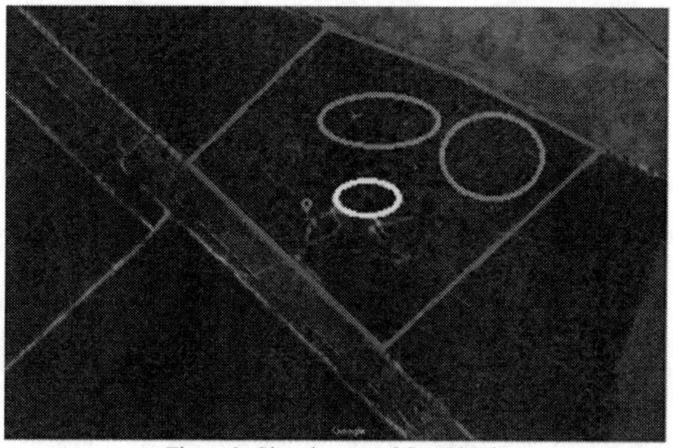

Figure 2: Closed space of Casabianda

We tested our GPS tracking system on a young male deer in this enclosure to validate its proof of concept (autonomy, real time visualization, long range communication and quick deployment).

A. The Network architecture

We propose to develop a basic architecture developed in two parts as showed on the Figure 3 :

1. Lora Antenna towards the monitored area : a LoRa tracker is integrated in a collar AMBLoRa. A LoRa network is deployed trough a KerlinK antenna ;
2. Lora Antenna towards the server database : a GSM connection allows a data transmission towards our data server.

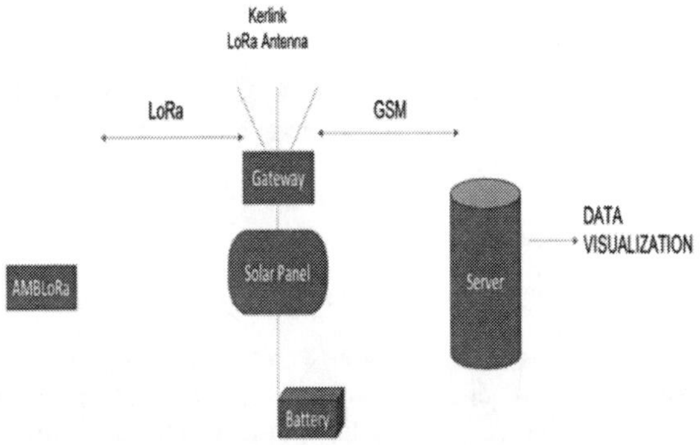

Figure 3 : Sytem architecture

B. The Lora Tracker

We designed a GPS tracking collar (Figure 4) using a classic hardware architecture of GPS tracking devices : a microcontroller, a battery, a network transmitter and a GPS. The embedded card is based on a microcontroller, a Microchip PIC24FJ128GA310.

This block, showed on Figure 5, receives the GPS location data, codifies and transmits this information to the data base with a LoRa transmitter. This module uses a high-performance, low-current Microchip RN2483. With a power supply of 3.6 V, the transceiver offers a sensitivity of -148 dBm and a maximum output power of +14 dBm, allowing long-distance communication at 868 MHz frequency

Our GPS receiver is an Origin GPS ORG1208. This block is the most energy-consuming with 100mA when it is working. But the fast position fix (± 5s) and the high sensitivity of -162dBm allows us to have low power consumption. We have also integrated an accelerometer into the embedded card (an Analog Devices Inc ADXL345) measuring the tagged animal activity. It allows to know if the tracking collar falls to the ground : loose collar or dead animal.

The GPS and GSM antennas of the AMBLoRa card were attached to the outside of the waterproof case using the collar. technology is used as wide area network wireless technology.

We can use different frequency bands defined (US 928 MHz, EU 863 MHz, China 787 MHz) ; it is a low power, long range and low data rate based technology developed with initiative by Semtech.

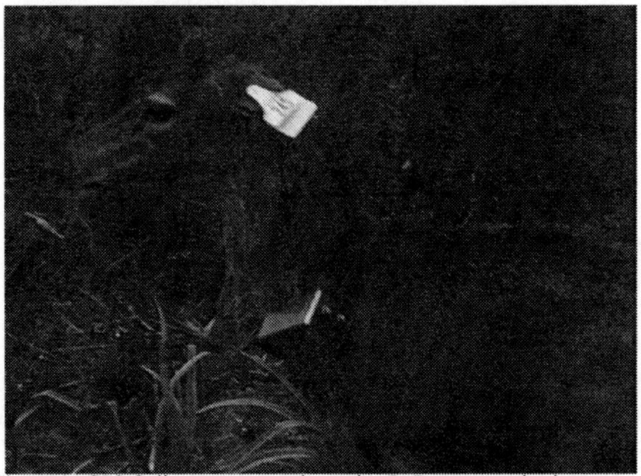

Figure 4 : GPS Collar on a young deer using LoRa communication

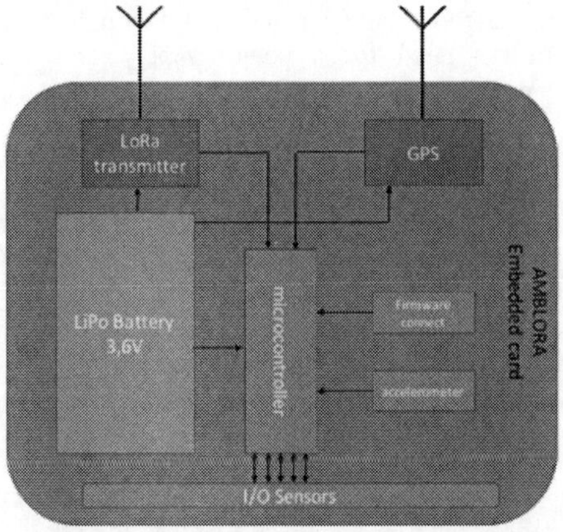

Figure 5 : block diagram of the proposed wireless embedded card

The main part of the embedded card is the microcontroller, a Microchip PIC24FJ128GA310. This block receives the location data from the GPS, codifies and transmits this information to the data base by using the LoRa transmitter.

C. Autonomous LoRa Network

All messages of the AMBLoRa card (ID, GPS position, accelerometer data, and time stamp) are transmitted to our servers via the LoRa network. We have deployed an antenna that covers the entire monitoring area. This antenna is autonomous in energy and communication network (Figure 6).

This gateway module is based on a high-performance, low-current Microchip RN2483. With a power supply of 3.6 V, the transceiver offers a sensitivity of -148 dBm and a maximum output power of +14 dBm, which allows long-distance communication at 868 MHz frequency.

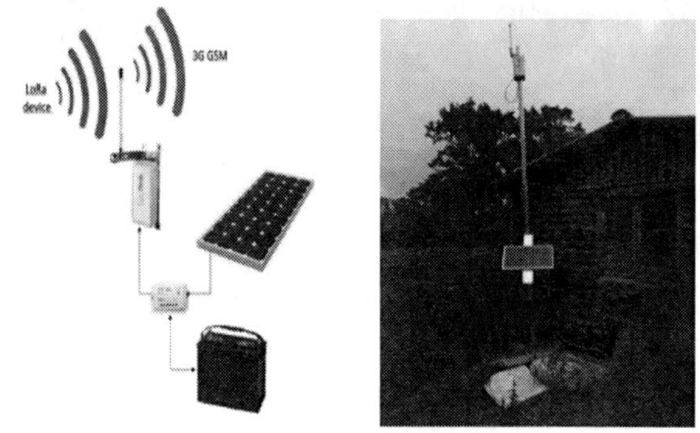

Figure 6 : autonomous LoRa antenna system

The autonomous antenna system consists of a EPsolar LandStar LS1024B PWM Solar Battery Charge Controller 10A 12/24V, a 25W solar panel, a lead acid battery 105Ah 12V and a Kerlink LoRa IoT Station. The Kerlink gateway uses the cellular network (2G/3G) to communicate with our servers [17].

The components we have used allows us to have a LoRa network gateway that we can deploy in a natural environment without the need for a power supply or communication network.

D. The relative real-time data vizualisation

The supervision software is available as a web application enabling users and administrators, among other things, to visualize the position of their devices. We made the choice to build a web application because we needed to access our data at any time on the largest number of devices. It offers four different services called real time, alerts, history and administration interface. Because it is the easiest way to display positions data on a screen, all data displaying is based on interactive maps. We also provide tables whose data can be exported.

The main purpose of the real time section is to display the latest position on the map of each individuals. We follow the positions of the fixed devices such as LoRa gateways are also available. Every target is represented by an interactive marker. The course shows the fifty latest positions as markers linked by lines that are dotted with arrows to indicate the direction.
The Web application is able to compute received data to extract useful information. By analyzing the target positions, we are able to determine if it is in trouble or not : for example a deer which is not moving during twenty-four hours. With these computed data the web application can emit alerts. Once an alert is emitted the corresponding marker on the real time section turns to red and it is visible into the alert section with more details available. Users can check alerts via a table which lists all current alerts and can acknowledge it. At the moment the system is able to issue alerts regarding the targets, the devices equipping these targets and the LoRa antennas. The web application enables us to be aware of the state of our facilities. We created the history section to store data and extract old courses.

The data produced by the devices must be stored to be accessible by the end users. We provide a very simple network architecture using two separate servers called respectively application server and database server. We used Laravel [18], a powerful and well documented PHP framework possessing a large community, to create both the web application and the API.

The supervision software (Figure 7) is available as a web application enabling users and administrators, among other things, to visualize the position of their devices.

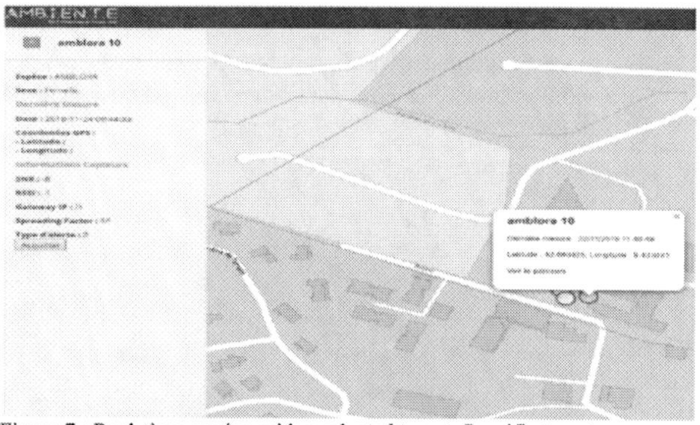

Figure 7 : Real-time section with a selected target. Specific target information is displayed into the sidebar. Popup gives restricted information and offers the possibilities to display the recent course of the target

We made the choice to build a web application because we needed to access our data at any time and on the largest number of mobile devices (smartphone). It offers four different services called real time, alerts, history and administration interface.

IV. First Results

In this part we present the first results of our experimentation according to two parts : data visualization and energy consumption.

A. Data visualization

The interpretation of the results is the last part of our work. We mainly worked with the historical section ; given that the deer was in a closed modest sized enclosure, it was not able to travel long distances. Its position belonging to a known interval, the real-time section was therefore useless. Hence we focused on studying its travels over short periods, ranging from 1 to 2 days, as well as on determining the most frequented places. Choosing a maximum gap of 2 days ensues from an obvious constraint. Considering the selected data sending frequency, it was not possible using the map to study the movement of the animal on a larger period of time, on such a small area, as this resulted in a mass of points and lines that could not be interpreted. We will see afterwards that another technique has been favored.

Nevertheless, as shown in the Figure 8, it is possible to study the animal behavior over the short term via our web application.

We can have a yellow point for each position of the dear after 10 minutes, determine a trajectory, and we can extract the history of a course for a post treatment of the data. For the longest periods of time, we have carried out a data export, still via our interface, in order to integrate them into a tools fitted software adapted to this amount of data. The following figure shows that it is not possible to extract a behavioral analysis from the raw data.

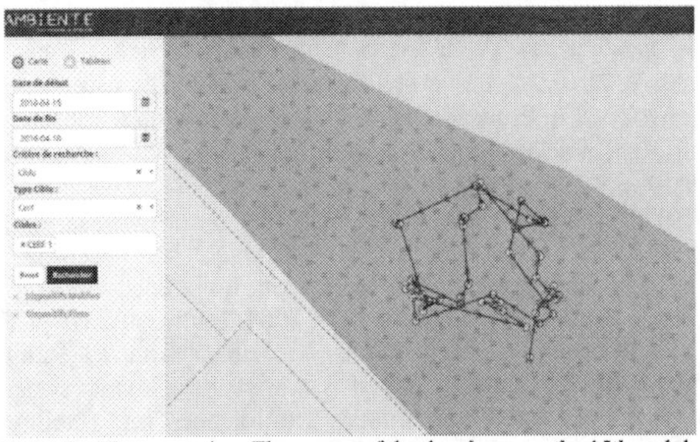

Figure 8 : History section. The course of the deer between the 15th and the 16th March

We requested to display all the geolocation data collected for the deer. It did not give us any useful information, besides it overloaded the web application making it slower to run, degrading the user's experience. We have found one of the limitations of using such a solution for animal tracking.

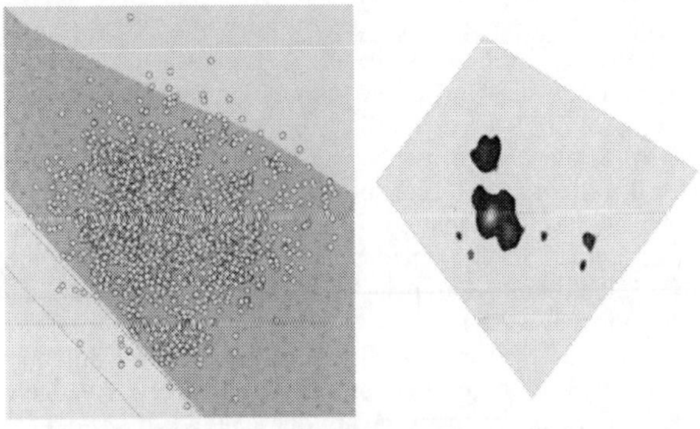

(a) (b)

Figure 9 : Data visualization (a) massive point representation (b) QGIS GIS analysis

On the Figure 9, (a) shows a massive amount of points which are the whole positions that we collected during our experimentations. (b) shows the corresponding heat map generated via QGIS highlighting the most frequented location. In order to overcome these limitations we imported the data into the QGIS GIS software. This enabled to generate heat maps from the data. Thanks to this map, we would highlight two areas : the closest to the hut, symbolized in green, is the area where the animal was fed and the cleared glade.

There are several advantages to have a real-time visualization of tracking data:

- Possibility to acquire remote positions (as, for example, for VHF tracking),
- Detection of abnormal behavior : short distance traveled, death of the animal, animal isolated from livestock, etc.
- Be alerted if an animal get out of a virtual enclosure (rambling, flight, etc.)

B. Energy consumption of AMBLoRa

In this part we introduce the first elements of energy consumption approach.

The Figure 10 shows the battery lifetime on the gateway and the charge level according to the sunshine. We can observe the robustness of the system. Figure 10 shows that the charge level of the battery used to power the LoRa gateway increases throughout the tracking, even if the sunshine is low for several days.

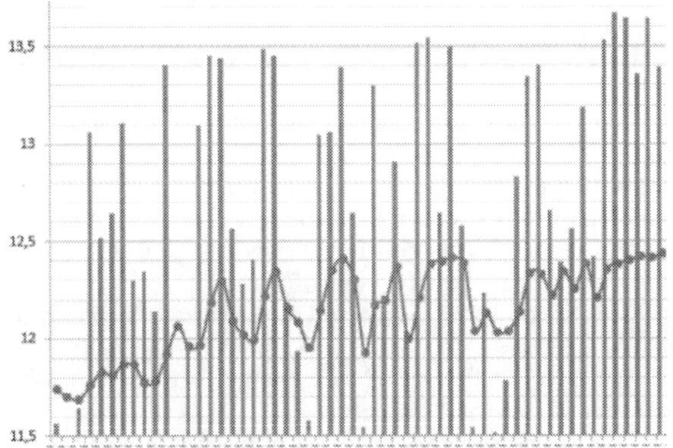

Figure 10 : daily average of the charge level of the antenna battery according to the sunshine (gray)

The energy consumption of the AMBLoRa card is an important issue for us. Our goal was to have a one year tracking time with one GPS location per hour. We can see on the Figure 11 the AMBLoRa battery life according to the number of GPS messages/hour.

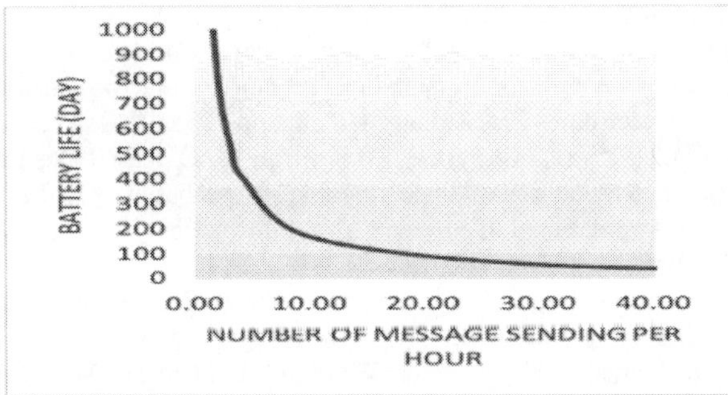

Figure 11 : Battery Lifetime of AMBLora

We measured the energy consumption of each component of the card when they are on, and also in standby. The GPS is the block that consumes the most during its fixed time with 90 to

100 mA. The LoRa transmitter consumes 12.8 mA during sending and all other components (microcontroller, accelerometer, etc.) not more than 1.4 mA. In standby, the GPS consumes less than 40μA, the LoRa module between 30 and 40μA, the microcontroller less than 10μA in "sleep-deep" mode and the accelerometer less than 1μA.
These performances allow us to consider up to 5 GPS position transmissions per hour for a tracking period of one year. For 1 GPS position transmission per hour, we can reach a follow-up period of 2 years.

V. Conclusion

AMBLoRa is a complete system that allows the researchers to visualize the relative real-time data from GPS tracking collar using LoRa communication, a designed low consumption support of communication. According to this first experiment, we conclude that AMBLoRa has achieved the four desired objectives : long range communication, low power consumption of the system, quick deployment and relative real time visualization. However we must enhance some parameters.

We get a position after a certain amount of time ; we can consider that it is a relative real time ; we must reduce the send period to minimum. But, there will always be a delay due to all the processes involved in the sending and displaying chain.

We only use one collar and it is essential to develop a massive experiment with more GPS trackers.

The size of AMBLoRa is still too large and we must reduce its size.

We must continue to reduce energy consumption, key of efficient animal tracking system.

We need to switch towards a LoRaWAN protocol in order to integrate a Medium Access Control optimized secured communication.

References

[1] A. Matthews, et al. "The success of GPS collar deployments on mammals in Australia". Australian Mammalogy 35, 2013, pp. 65-83.

[2] M. Saari, A. Muzaffar bin Baharudin, P. Sillberg, S. Hyrynsalmi and W. Yan, "LoRa - A Survey of Recent Research Trends" 41st International Convention on Information and Communication Technology, Electronics and Microelectronics Proceedings, Croatia, pp 1035-1040, 2018

[3] D. H. Kim, J. B. Park, J. H. Shin, and J. D. Kim, "Design and implementation of object tracking system based on LoRa," 2017 International Conference on Information Networking (ICOIN), pp.463–467, 2017.

[4] L. Li, J. Ren, and Q. Zhu, "On the application of LoRa LPWAN technology in Sailing Monitoring System," 2017 13th Annual Conference on Wireless On-Demand Network Systems and Services, WONS 2017 - Proceedings, pp. 77–80, 2017.

[5] W. San-Um, P. Lekbunyasin, M. Kodyoo, W. Wongsuwan, J. Makfak, and J. Kerdsri, "A long-range low-power wireless sensor network based on U-LoRa technology for tactical troops tracking systems," in 2017 Third Asian Conference on Defence Technology (ACDT). IEEE, pp. 32–35, 2017

[6] B. C. Fargas and M. N. Petersen, "GPS-free geolocation using LoRa in low-power WANs," in 2017 Global Internet of Things Summit (GIoTS). IEEE, pp. 1–6, 2017.

[7]http://sirtrack.co.nz/index.php/terrestrialmain/gps/collar retrieved: May 2018

[8]https://www.telemetrysolutions.com/wildlife-tracking-devices/gps-collars/ retrieved: April 2018

[9] R. Zviedris, A. Elsts, G. Strazdins, A. Mednis, and L. Selavo. 2010. "LynxNet: wild animal monitoring using sensor networks." In Proceedings of the 4th international conference on Real-world wireless sensor networks (REALWSN'10), 2010, pp. 170-173.

[10] P. Zhang, C. M. Sadler, S. A. Lyon and M. Martonosi, "Hardware design experiences in ZebraNet", Proceedings of the 2nd international conference on Embedded networked sensor systems, November 03-05, 2004, Baltimore, MD, USA

[11] R. Bagree, V. R. Jain, A. Kumar and P. Ranjan, "wildCENSE: GPS based animal tracking system" Proceedings of International Conference on Intelligent Sensors, Sensor Networks and Information Processing, 2008.

[12] E. D. Ayele, N. Meratnia and P. J. M. Havinga. "Towards A New Opportunistic IoT Network Architecture for Wildlife Monitoring System" Proceeding of 9th IFIP International Conference on New Technologies, Mobility and Security (NTMS), 2018, Paris, France.

[13] N. Kidjo, et al. (2007). Extirpation and reintroduction of the Corsican red deer Cervus elaphus corsicanus in Corsica. Oryx, 41(4), 488.

[14] http://www.pnr.corsica/grande-faune/ May 2018

[15] LoRa Alliance. White Paper: A Technical Overview of Lora and Lorawan; The LoRa Alliance: San Ramon, CA, USA, 2015

[16] M. Printice, et al. Enabling Miniature Position Tracker Using LoRa and GPS Technology. European Conference on Antennas and Propagation (EuCAP), Apr 2016, Davos, Switzerland. CS09.1: Antenna for IoT applications (2905-2908), 2016, Proc. European Conference on Antennas and Propagation (EuCAP).

[17] LoRa IoT Station 868 MHz - Kerlink | M2m : Solutions de communication machinetomachine. [Online]. Available: https://www.thethingsnetwork.org/docs/gateways/kerlink/ (visited on Mar. 26 2018)

[18] https://laravel.com/ retrieved: April 2018

Ultra-wideband Indoor Positioning Based on Triangle Midpoint Algorithm

Wen Piao Lin
Dept. of Electrical Engineering
Chang Gung University
Tao-Yuan, Taiwan
e-mail: wplin@mail.cgu.edu.tw

Yu-Fang Hsu
Dept. of Electronic Engineering
Chienkuo Technology University
Changhua, Taiwan
e-mail: yfshi@ctu.edu.tw

***Abstract*—In this paper, we present an experimental indoor positioning system consisting of three anchor nodes and a tag, which uses a microprocessor with an ultra-wideband wireless transceiver device. The scheme based on the time-of-arrival technique and triangle midpoint algorithm provides accurate localization in a limited indoor area. The average localization error of the proposed positioning system placed in the indoor space of 732cm×488cm×220cm is 12.87cm. The experimental results demonstrated that the proposed system has the characteristics of high precision localization and less computation time.**

Keywords-indoor positioning; ultra-wideband (UWB); time-of-arrival (TOA); triangle midpoint algorithm(TMA).

I. INTRODUCTION

Many different positioning technologies are applied to the indoor environment for research, including Radio Frequency Identification Devices (RFID) [1][2], infrared sensors [3], Zigbee [4], Wireless Networks (Wi-Fi) [5], low Power Bluetooth [6] and so on. These different technologies are usually selected from the Received Signal Strength Indicator (RSSI) to achieve indoor positioning. Signals are relatively easy to be blocked by objects and cause poor penetration. They are easily affected by multiple path interferences, and the accuracy is mostly low. Therefore, it is necessary to set multiple reference points in the indoor environment or build the database in advance to improve the indoor positioning accuracy.

Ultra-wideband (UWB) wireless transmission technology has excellent transmission quality in complex indoor environments and has the advantages of high transmission speed, excellent resistance to multi-path interference, low power, high penetration, and high time accuracy [7]-[9]. UWB transceiver utilizes a very short Radio Frequency (RF) pulse to achieve high bandwidth connections. It can execute an accurate measurement of time delay and distance difference [9][10]. Many algorithms for UWB indoor positioning have been proposed such as calculating the Time-Of-Arrival (TOA) or Time-Difference-Of-Arrival (TDOA) schemes [12]. From the above, it is known that UWB is quite suitable for indoor positioning, and the positioning accuracy is high, even reaching a minimum error of 10 cm.

This research mainly uses a microprocessor to control UWB device, and then uses TOA triangulation method, combined with a fast positioning Triangle Midpoint Algorithm (TMA) to implement an accuracy indoor positioning system. First, a single tag based on a single base station measures its positioning accuracy and Environmental Parameter Calibration (EPC). After that, three base stations are placed in the three corners of the laboratory space, and the distances of the tags are respectively captured to test the arrival time method. Finally, the test results input into computer to evaluate and explore the positioning accuracy and computation time.

This paper is organized as follows; the indoor wireless positioning system is presented in Section II. Then, the UWB positioning scheme is briefly explained in Section III. After that, the implementation of the positioning algorithm is described in Section IV. Then, experimental setup and results are discussed in Section V. Finally, Section VI concludes the paper.

II. INDOOR WIRELESS POSITIONING SYSTEM

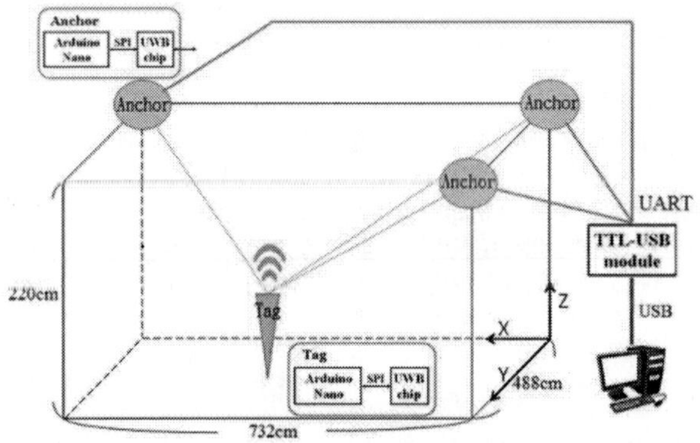

Figure. 1. Block diagram of UWB Indoor wireless location system

Figure 1 is a block diagram of UWB indoor wireless positioning system. The green ellipse is the base station that is an anchor. In the middle of the figure, the gray inverted triangle is a tag to be located. The base station is placed in three corners of the experimental space and connected to the computer using Universal Asynchronous Receiver and Transmitter (UART) through a Transistor-Transistor Logic-Universal Serial Bus (TTL-USB) module. Then the measured data are written in JAVA programming language of TOA triangulation positioning scheme, and finally by the coordinate system to calculate a positioning point and its error for real-time operation. The tag and anchors are integrated by the Arduino microprocessor with a UWB device (DW1000) as shown in the inset of Figure 1. The control program is programming in the microprocessor and communicates with the UWB device via the Serial Peripheral Interface Bus (SPIB). The base station and the tag are a wireless signal transmission using ultra-wideband pulses.

The DW1000 [13] is a single chip radio transceiver Integrated Circuit (IC) compliant with the IEEE 802.15.4-2011 UWB standard. It facilitates real time location of assets into an accuracy of +/- 10 cm using either two-way ranging TOA measurements or one-way TDOA schemes. Moreover, DW1000 spans 6 radio frequency bands from 3.5 GHz to 6.5 GHz and also supports data rates of 110 kbps, 850 kbps and 6.8 Mbps. The transmitting or receiving signal for the DW1000 is used as a semi-directive antenna. The signal will be transmitted in an arc towards the antenna's facing side. This means that the back of the antenna has poor signal. It is a factor that affects the accuracy of the distance measurement on the anchor and needs to be taken into account.

III. UWB Positioning Scheme

This section describes various methods of implementing UWB two-way ranging scheme between two nodes. In all of the schemes that follow one node acts as initiator, initiating a range measurement, while the other node acts as a responder listening and responding to the initiator, and calculating the range.

A. *Single-sided Two-way Ranging*

Single-Sided Two-Way Ranging (SS-TWR) involves a simple measurement of the round trip delay of a single message from one node to another and a response sent back to the original node. The operation of SS-TWR is as shown in Figure 2, where Tag initiates the exchange and Anchor A responds to complete the exchange and each device precisely timestamps the transmission and reception times of the message frames, and so can calculate time $T_{round\ A}$, and $T_{reply\ A}$, by simple subtraction. The resultant TOA, T_{prorA}, may be estimated by the equation:

$$T_{propA} = \frac{1}{2}\left(T_{roundA} - T_{replyA}\right) \quad (1)$$

and then multiplied by the speed of light c can be obtained the distance D_A between the two devices:

$$D_A = T_{propA} \times C \quad (2)$$

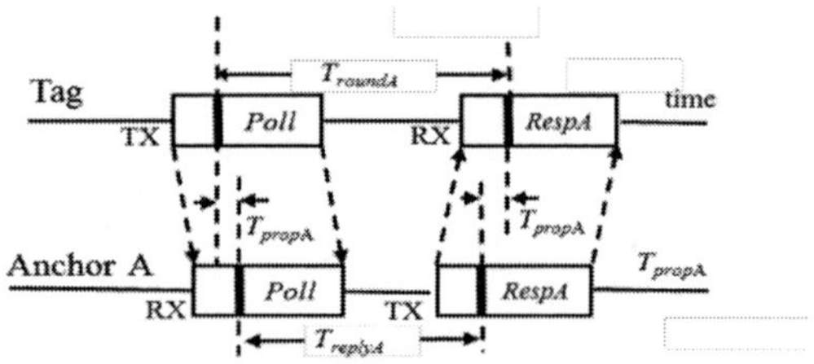

Figure. 2. Single station SS-TWR scheme

B. *Double-sided Two-way Ranging*

Double-Sided Two-Way Ranging (DS-TWR), is an extension of the basic SS-TWR in which two round trip time measurements are used and combined to give a TOA result which has a reduced error even for quite long response delays. Figure 3 shows the DS-TWR of multiple stations for single tag [13]. It can be seen in the graph that the tag sends a poll message which is received by three anchors in the infrastructure who reply in successive responses with packets RespA, RespB and RespC after which the tag sends the Final message received by all three anchors. This allows the tag to be located after sending only 2 messages and receiving 3. Anchor A and the tag can calculate the corresponding time T_{propA}, and then multiplied by the speed of light c can be obtained the distance D_A between the two devices:

$$T_{propA} = \frac{\left(T_{round1A} \times T_{round2A} - T_{reply1A} \times T_{reply2A}\right)}{\left(T_{round1A} + T_{round2A} + T_{reply1A} + T_{reply2A}\right)} \quad (3)$$

$$D_A = T_{propA} \times C \quad (4)$$

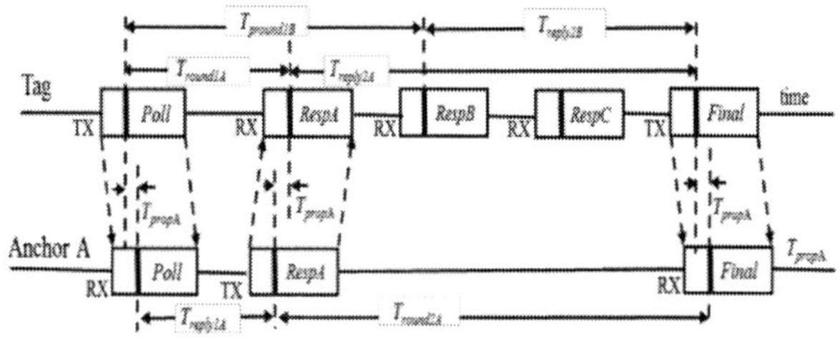

Figure. 3. Multiple station DS-TWR scheme

Similarly, between anchor B, anchor C and the tag can calculate the corresponding time T_{prorB} and T_{prorC}, and then multiplied by the speed of light c can be obtained the distance of D_B and D_C between the two devices.

IV. Positioning Algorithm

The concept of the Triangle Centroid Algorithm (TCA) was first proposed by Prof. Nirupama Bulusu of the University of Southern California [14]. The main reason is that if unknown nodes can receive signals from N anchor nodes, unknown nodes can consider as anchor nodes and the triangle centroid of the polygons formed by overlapping places [15]. However, the actual space has a high degree of complexity. In the real environment, the distance from the tag to the base station is slightly larger than the actual value. The circle drawn according to the TOA method not only intersects at one point but overlaps with the triangle area in the figure. Figure 4 shows the principle diagram of TCA where A, B, C are base stations, and T is the target tag.

The three-circle intersections obtained from the TOA method in all cases can locate in the same triangle as the previous section, and the target can estimate by triangle centroid algorithm. When F anchor leaves far away, the area of the three-circle interaction will not approximate as a triangle-shaped DEF. When TCA is used to estimate the target coordinates, the accuracy will decrease because of too narrow triangles. Therefore, we propose a TOA Triangle Midpoint Algorithm (TMA) to improve positioning accuracy.

From Figure 4, we can speculate that the tag position will be very close to the arc DF and arc EF so that the tag will fall in the upper right corner of the yellow area near the arc DE. Here, we propose to use the point M of the intersection DE as the method of positioning coordinates to improve the error of the TCA.

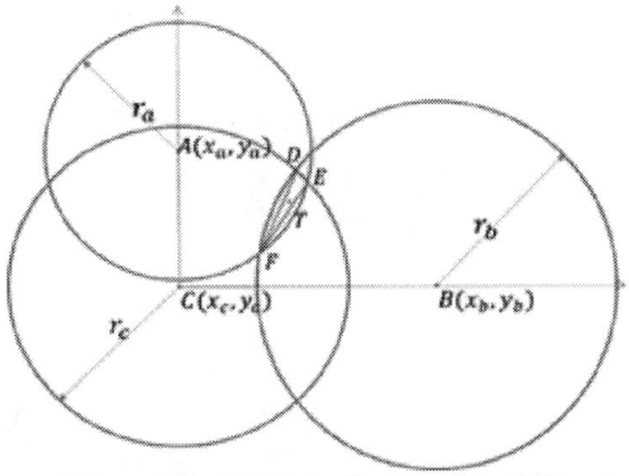

Figure. 4. The Principle diagram of the TCA

The coordinates of $D(x_d, y_d)$ shown in the Figure 3 can be inferred from the triangle formula

$$\sqrt{(x_d - x_a)^2 + (y_d - y_a)^2} \le r_a$$
$$\sqrt{(x_d - x_b)^2 + (y_d - y_b)^2} = r_b \qquad (5)$$
$$\sqrt{(x_d - x_c)^2 + (y_d - y_c)^2} = r_c$$

Similarly, the coordinates of $E(x_e, y_e)$ are derived. Finally, we find the coordinates of the midpoint $M(x_m, y_m)$ of arc DE as coordinates of the target after positioning:

$$x_m = \frac{x_d + x_e}{2}, \quad y_m = \frac{y_d + y_e}{2} \qquad (6)$$

The TMA software processing flow is shown in Figure 5. When the base station starts up, it will enter the standby state and determine whether there is a message in the tag. If no signal is received, it will continue to standby. Otherwise, the base station will synchronize with the tag. After bi-directional ranging performs after synchronization, the distance data is obtained. The TOA positioning calculation is performed using the JAVA programming language. The next step is to establish a coordinate system and place the three groups of base station positions as the center of the circle at the origin (0, 0), the X-axis point (X, 0) and the Y-axis point (0, Y). The distances measured by the three groups of base stations and tags plot as a radius, and then the TMA is used to locate and calculate the intersection points D and E between the origin circle and the other two circles. Second, calculate the midpoint M between the two points D and E, and finally, use M as the positioning coordinate. After ending the algorithm, determine if the tag is offline. If the tag is disconnected, the base station returns to the standby state. If the tag continues to transmit, the bidirectional ranging is continued.

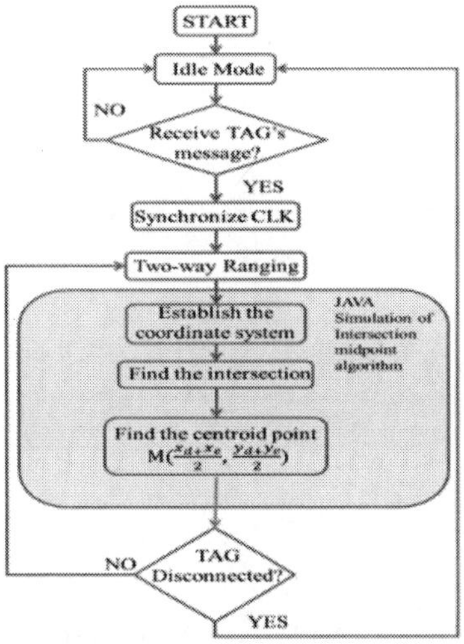

Figure. 5. Flow chart of TMA scheme

V. Experimental Setup and Results

In this experiment, a 12×8 coordinate system was established on a lab room space of 732cm×488cm×220cm by a 61cm×61cm square grid on the ceiling. The base station placed in the three corners of the lab and connected it to the computer, and then measure the distance of the tag unilaterally as shown in Figure 1. The measured distance is estimated by the of the computer positioning algorithm. Finally, the positioning error is calculated by the coordinate system.

A. *One-to-One Ranging Test*

One-to-one obstacle-free distance test between devices was first performed. The measured actual distance starts from 50 cm, and then an experiment is conducted every 50 cm. The test results were recorded, and 30 test values were averaged as test values until the actual distance was up to 10 m. A total of 20 one-to-one accessibility measurements are performed. Figure 6 is the error calculated from the one-to-one accessibility test value versus actual value. It can be found that the error is less than 6% at a distance which is less than 6 m. The converted error is approximately 20 to 30 cm. When the distance is more than 6 meters, the error starts to increase gradually.

Since the one-to-one ranging distance between devices directly affects the positioning accuracy, we correct the measured values from 0.5m to 10m interval for every 0.5m. The value is corrected as the demarcation point between the minimum value of the subsequent segment and the maximum value of the previous segment; for example, the average value of 30-data measured at distance of 6.5m is 6.889m, and the minimum value is 6.68m. The measured error is 0.389m. Next, the maximum value of 30-data measured at distance of 6m is 6.39m. Therefore, we can calculate that the demarcation point will be (6.68+6.39)/2 =6.54m. When the measured distance is greater than 6.54 m, the measured value must be deducted 0.389m. The error of the one-to-one distance test after correction is about 0.1m, and the accuracy is much improved.

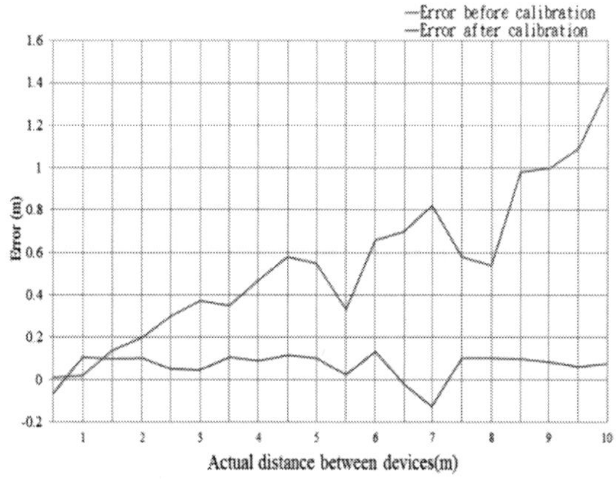

Figure. 6. Calibration of localization error

The height of the tag on the Z axis will affect the accuracy of the distance measurement. When the distance between two nodes on the XY plane is 6m, the error is 0.082m under the height of 1m on the Z axis. And when the distance between two nodes is 1m, the error is 0.414m under the height of 1m on the Z axis. Therefore, in order to improve the accuracy of the three-dimension measurement, tag position should be as far as possible with three anchors in the same plane.

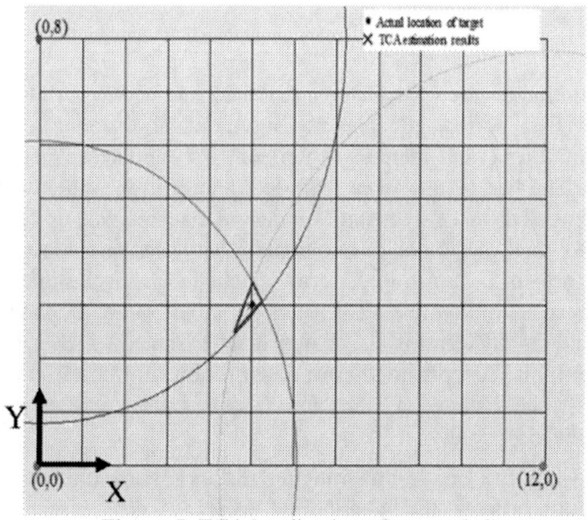

Figure. 7. TCA localization of tag at (5, 3)

B. TCA Localization Test

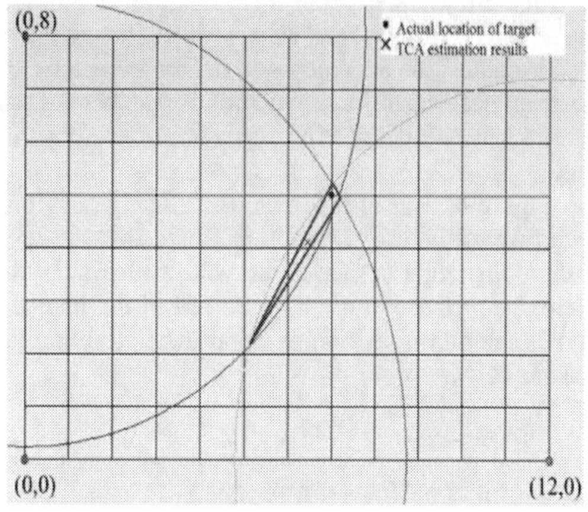

Figure. 8. TCA localization of tag at (7, 5)

TABLE I. LOCALIZATION ERROR FOR VARIOUS ALGORITHMS

Coordinates	Error (cm) of triangle centroid algorithm	Error(cm) of triangle midpoint algorithm	Error (cm) of inner triangle centroid algorithm
(1,2)	23	26.19	20.22
(3,1)	3.31	10.85	10.84
(3,6)	24.3	8.048	7.88
(5,3)	1.92	16.99	14.58
(7,3)	19.95	13.59	12.11
(7,5)	63.68	8.57	8.54
(10,7)	188.45	14.48	14.48
(11,3)	80.49	10.03	9.98
(11,5)	145.55	6.93	6.93
(12,6)	202.96	13	12.92
Average error (cm)	75.36	12.87	11.85
Standard deviation	72.91	5.36	3.76

We placed three base stations on the origin (0, 0), Y-axis (0, 8), and X-axis (12, 0); the tag is placed at different points in the coordinates. When a positioning coordinate of the tag is located at (5, 3) shown in Figure 7, the calculated positioning coordinate after TCA execution is (4.97, 2.99). The error is converted to approximately 1.92 cm; however, when the positioning coordinate of the tag is located at (7, 5) shown in Figure 8, the calculated positioning coordinate after TCA execution is (6.43, 4.12). The actual error is converted to approximately 63.68 cm. Finally, when the positioning coordinate of the tag is located at (11, 5), the calculated coordinate after TCA is (9.73, 2.98). The actual error is converted to about 145.55 cm. From test results when the tag is located far away from the XY coordinates, the positioning using the TCA scheme will be invalid. The main reason is that the triangle completed by the TCA is too narrow, resulting in the measurement error is greater when the tag is far away from the XY coordinates. The detailed experimental results of 10 coordinate points by TCA scheme are shown in Table 1.

C. TMA Localization Test

To solve the problem when the tag is placed on the X and Y coordinates with larger values, the triangle is too narrow and long to decrease accuracy shown in Figure 8. Therefore, we propose a solution for the midpoint of the triangle. The intersection of the red circle and the blue circle and the intersection of the red circle and the green circle are selected, and the middle point is taken as the rear coordinate after positioning shown in Figure 9. This can avoid the large change of the blue circle and the green circle.

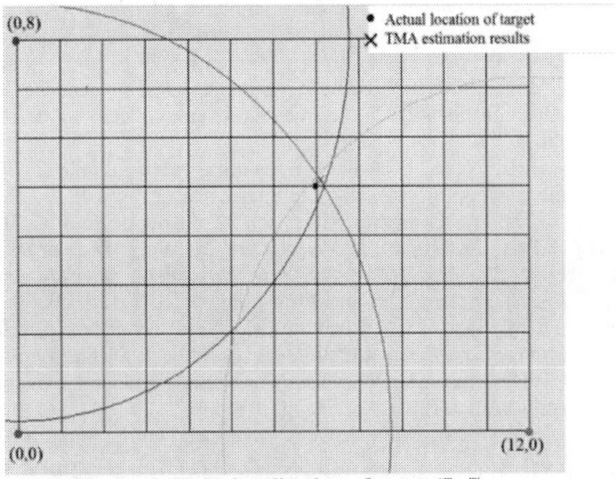

Figure. 9. TMA localization of tag at (7, 5)

When a positioning coordinate of the tag is located at (7, 5) shown in Figure 9, the calculated positioning coordinate is (7.09, 5.1). The error is converted to about 8.57 cm. When the positioning coordinate of the tag is located at (11, 5) shown in Figure 10, the calculated positioning coordinate is (11.1, 5.04), and the error is converted to about 6.93 cm. The detailed experimental results of 10 coordinate points by TMA scheme are shown in Table 1.

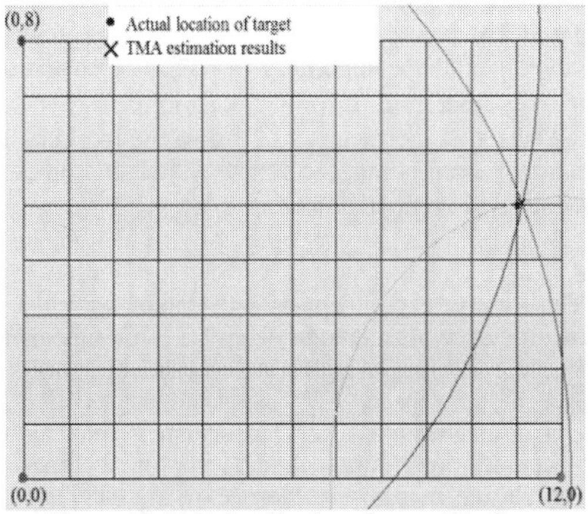

Figure. 10. TMA localization of tag at (11, 5)

D. Comparison of Algorithm

To understand the performance of proposed TMA, we write a computer program to compare localization error for various algorithms. The Inner Triangle Centroid Algorithm (ITCA) [16] published by Nantong University of China. The comparison error is the distance between the coordinates of the tag calculated by each algorithm and the actual position of the target. A total of ten points in the ordinates take for ranging experiments. Finally, the average error and standard deviation figure out. It can be seen from Table 1 that the accuracy of the ITCA is the highest with an average error of approximately 11.848 cm. The accuracy of

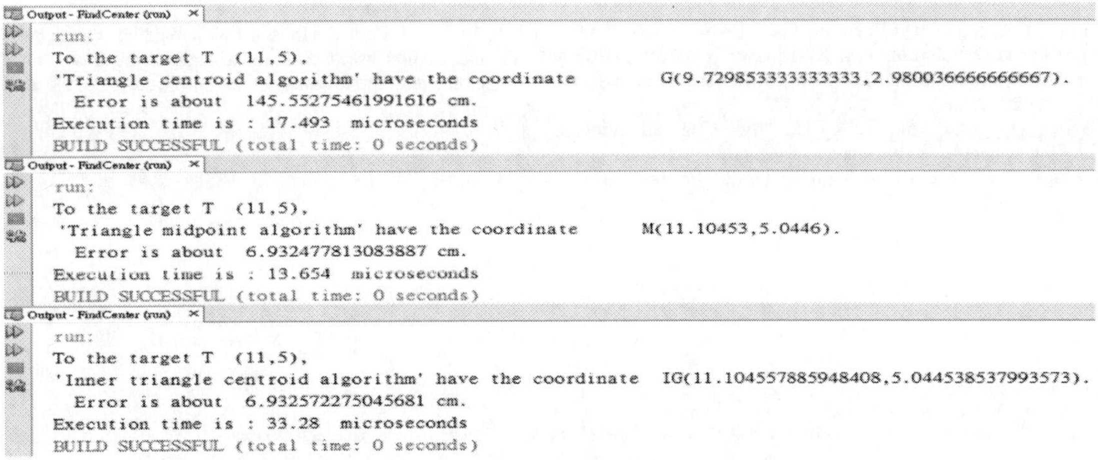

Figure. 11. Computation time for different algorithms

TMA is slightly lower than that of the ITCA. The average error is about 12.869 cm. Moreover, the TCA performs well in some coordinates at the positioning (3, 1) and positioning (5, 3). However, when the target is farther away from the origin, the TCA cannot accurately locate the target. The average error is 75.36 cm.

The computation time of the algorithm at the positioning (11, 5) shown in Fig. 11 that the algorithm of the proposed TMA is simple and requires only 13.654 μs for positioning; and the algorithm of ITCA is comparatively complexity, therefore, takes 33.28 μs to execute it once. It can be seen that the accuracy of proposed algorithm is very high. At the same time, the simple calculation process can be reduced the computation time.

VI. CONCLUSION

This study experimented and demonstrated a high-precision indoor positioning system based on time-of-arrival technique and triangle midpoint localization algorithm in a limited indoor space. We characterized existing ultra-wideband localization algorithm schemes and explored a high-accuracy algorithm method. According to experimental results that the accuracy of the one-to-one ranging between the anchor and a tag is almost within 10 cm. Moreover, the average error of the ultra-wideband positioning systems is about 12.87 cm to use the triangle midpoint localization algorithm in a laboratory space of 732cm×488cm×220cm. Finally, we also compare the execution time of various positioning algorithms. The experimented results show that the proposed algorithm has a simple calculation process which can reduce the computation time and reach a real-time process.

The security aspects in the positioning can be treated at the positioning algorithm. Cryptographic techniques could be used for improving the security and privacy of location information in the actual applications. This issue still largely lacks sufficient solutions and can be expected as a future work item.

REFERENCES

[1] X. Liu, M. Wen, G. Qin, and R. Liu, "LANDMARC with improved k-nearest algorithm for RFID location system", IEEE International Conference on Computer and Communications, pp. 2569-2572, 2016.

[2] S. Sahin, H. Ozcan, and K. Kucuk, "SmartTag: an indoor positioning system based on smart transmit power scheme using active tags", IEEE Access, vol. 6, pp. 23500 -23510, Mar. 2018.

[3] Y. Kobiyama, Q. Zhao, and K. Omomo "Privacy preserving infrared sensor array based indoor location awareness", IEEE International Conference on Systems, Man, and Cybernetics, pp. 001353-001358, 2016.

[4] C. H. Chu, et al., "High-accuracy indoor personnel tracking system with a zigbee wireless sensor network", Seventh International Conference on Mobile Ad-hoc and Sensor Networks, pp. 398-402, 2011.

[5] X. Ge and Z. Qu, "Optimization WIFI indoor positioning KNN algorithm location-based fingerprint", 7th IEEE International Conference on Software Engineering and Service Science, pp. 135-137, 2016.

[6] M. E. Rida, F. Liu, Y. Jadi, A. Algawhari, and A. Askourih, "Indoor location position based on bluetooth signal strength", 2nd International Conference on Information Science and Control Engineering, pp. 769-773, 2015.

[7] S. Gezici, Z. Tian, and G. B. Giannakis, "Localization via ultra-wideband radios: a look at positioning aspects for future sensor networks", IEEE Signal Processing Magazine, vol. 22, no. 4, pp. 70-84, 2005.

[8] D. B. Jourdan, D. Dardari, and M.Z. Win, "Position error bound for UWB localization in dense cluttered environments", IEEE Transactions on Aerospace and Electronic Systems, vol. 44, no. 2, pp. 613-628, 2008.

[9] D. Munoz, F. Bouchereau, C. vargas, and R. Enriquez-Caldera, "Position location techniques and applications", Academic Press, Elsevier Inc., 2009.

[10] S. Gezici, et al., "Localization via ultra-wideband radios: a look at positioning aspects for future sensor networks", IEEE Signal Processing Magazine, vol. 22, no. 4, pp. 70–84, 2005.

[11] C. Falsi, D. Dardari, L. Mucchi, and M. Win, "Time of arrival estimation for UWB localizers in realistic environments", Journal on Applied Signal Processing, pp. 152–152, 2006.

[12] M. M. Saad, C. J. Bleakley, M. Walsh, and T. Ye, "High accuracy location estimation for a mobile tag using one-way UWB signaling", Ubiquitous Positioning, Indoor Navigation, and Location Based Service, pp.1-8, 2012.

[13] DW1000 User Manual, DecaWave Ltd, Dublin, version 2.05, 2015.

[14] N. Bulusu, J. Heidemann, and D. Estrin, "GPS-less Low cost outdoor localization for very small devices", IEEE Personal Communications Magazine, vol.7, no.5, pp.28-34, 2000.

[15] Z.-M. Wang and Y. Zheng, "The study of the weighted centroid localization algorithm based on RSSI", International Conference on Wireless Communication and Sensor Network, pp. 276-279, Dec. 2014.

[16] W. Pei, J. Ping, J. He, and H. Zhang, "Ultra-wideband indoor localization based on inner triangle centroid algorithm", J. of Computer Applications, vol. 37, no. 1 pp. 289-293, 2017.

Layered Modeling Approach for Distributed Situation Recognition in Smart Environments

Mathias Mormul, Pascal Hirmer, Matthias Wieland, and Bernhard Mitschang

Institute of Parallel and Distributed Systems
University of Stuttgart, Universitätsstr. 38, D-70569, Germany
email: firstname.lastname@ipvs.uni-stuttgart.de

Abstract—**In the last decade, multiple new paradigms changed the way IT works. Cloud and Edge Computing led to new approaches, such as Smart Factories and Smart Cities, but also to new challenges and opportunities. One of those challenges is the recognition of situations, e.g., machine failures. Especially in the domain of industrial manufacturing, several requirements have to be met in order to deliver a reliable and efficient situation recognition. One of these requirements is distribution. The main contribution of this paper is a layered modeling approach for modeling situations to enable the distribution of situation recognition based on distribution patterns that are introduced in this paper.**

Keywords–Industry 4.0; Edge Computing; Smart Factories; Smart Homes; Situation Recognition; Distribution Pattern.

I. INTRODUCTION

In recent years, Industry 4.0 (I4.0), the digitization of the manufacturing industry, emerges as a new paradigm enabling approaches, such as Smart Factories [1]. In I4.0, devices equipped with sensors and actuators communicate with each other through uniform network addressing schemes to reach common goals [2][3]. Oftentimes, this goal is situation recognition, which enables monitoring of I4.0 environments and, consequently, the timely reaction to occurring situations. For example, the occurrence of a traffic accident in a Smart City, recognized by sensors of a vehicle, could lead to an adaptation of traffic lights to control the affected traffic.

Situations are recognized through the aggregation of con text data which, in I4.0, is usually provided by sensors. In current approaches, such as the one we introduced in our previous work [4][5], situations are recognized in a monolithic IT infrastructure in the cloud. Consequently, involved context data needs to be shipped to the processing infrastructure in order to recognize situations. However, especially in domains where efficiency is of vital importance, e.g., Smart Factories, this approach is not feasible. In order to fulfill important requirements, such as low network latency and fast response times, the situation recognition needs to be conducted as close to the context data sources as possible and, therefore, in a distributed manner. Processing data close to the sources is commonly known as Edge Computing [6].

In this paper, we introduce an approach to enable a distributed situation recognition. By doing so, we introduce so-called *distribution patterns*. These patterns represent common ways to distribute the recognition of situations, i.e., exclusively in the *edge*, in on-premise or off-premise cloud infrastructures, or based on a hybrid approach. We provide a layered approach for modeling and executing the situation recognition based on these distribution patterns. Our approach builds on a set of requirements we derive from a use case scenario in the manufacturing domain. We validate the approach by applying it to our previous non-distributed situation recognition [4][5] that is based on the modeling and execution of so-called Situation Templates [7].

The remainder of this paper is structured as follows: Section II describes related work and foundational background. In Section III, we introduce a motivating scenario, which is used to derive requirements for our approach. In Section IV, we present the main contribution of our paper. Finally, Section V concludes the paper and gives an outlook to future work.

II. RELATED WORK AND BACKGROUND

In this section, we describe related work, as well as foundational concepts of our previous work that are necessary to comprehend our approach.

A. Related Work

In related work, approaches exist for distributed situation recognition using ontologies, e.g., Fang et al. [8]. These approaches do not achieve the latency required in real-time critical scenarios, such as Industry 4.0 [1], due to time-consuming reasoning. The goal of our approach is to offer a low latency for distributed situation recognition in the range of milliseconds. Many approaches using ontologies are in the range of seconds to minutes, even without distribution [9][10]. Using machine learning leads to similar limitations regarding latency [11].

In the area of distributed Complex Event Processing (CEP), Schilling et al. [12] aim at integrating different CEP systems using a common meta language. This allows to use different CEP systems and integrate the results. This could be beneficial for our distribution because we would not be limited to one execution environment. However, in [12], the queries have to be hand-written and distributed. This is difficult, especially for domain experts, e.g., in Industry 4.0, who do not have computer science knowledge. In our approach, we provide an abstraction by Situation Templates that can be modeled using a graphical user interface. Furthermore, the users are supported in splitting up the template and in the distribution decision. Other approaches in distributed CEP, e.g., by Schultz-Moller et al. [13], follow the concept of automatic query rewriting. Here, CEP queries are split up using automated rewriting and are distributed on different operators based on a cost model, which is mostly based on CPU usage in the different nodes. In our approach, we want to support the user to select the desired

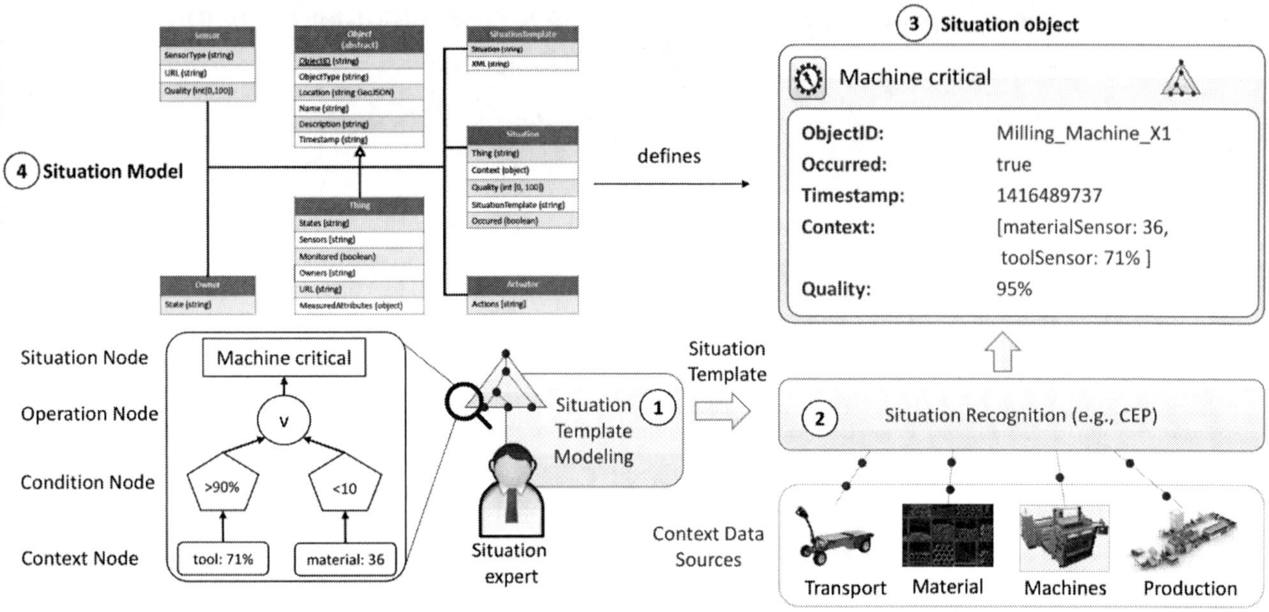

Figure 1. Previous approach for situation recognition

distribution type. Since there are many aspects, such as data protection or security, that play a role in distributing the CEP queries correctly, this only can be known by a responsible user.

Furthermore, approaches exist that enable a massive distribution of sensors, e.g., by Laerhoven and Gellersen [14] in cloths, to detect activities of the person wearing the cloth. This is similar to detecting the situation in the edge, but there is no concept presented in [14] to integrate the activities with other activities from different edges or create a global situation involving different locations.

B. Background

In this section, we describe our previous work. Our first approach for situation recognition, this paper builds on, is depicted in Figure 1. This approach is a result of the issues of related work, as discussed in the previous section.

An important fundamental concept are Situation Templates (ST), introduced by Häussermann et al. [7]. We adapted the STs in [5] to model and recognize situations. Situation Templates (see Figure 1 on the buttom left) consist of *context, condition* and *operation* nodes, which are used to model specific situations. Context nodes describe the input for the situation recognition, i.e., the context data, based on the definition of Dey et al. [15]. Context nodes are connected to condition nodes, which define the conditions that have to apply for a situation to be valid. Operation nodes combine condition and operation nodes and represent the logical operators *AND, OR*, or *XOR*. Operation nodes are used to aggregate all condition nodes of the ST into a single node, the situation node.

After modeling of a ST (Figure 1, Step 1), we developed a transformation into an executable representation (not depicted) was realized using CEP or light-weight execution languages, such as Node-RED. The advantage of this transformation is that it provides a flexible means to recognize situations. These transformations can be found in [16][17]. Consequently, we are not limited to specific engines or data formats. Once the transformation is done, the executable Situation Template is handed over to the corresponding execution engine.

On execution (Figure 1, Step 2), context data originating from the context sources is validated against the conditions defined by the Situation Template, for example, through pattern recognition in CEP. On each validation, we create a so-called situation object [18], defining whether the situation occurred and containing the involved context data (Figure 1, Step 3). We created a Situation Model [18](Figure 1, Step 4) to define the attributes of those situation objects. This leads to a better understanding of how context data led to the situation.

This previous approach for situation recognition works well, however, there are still some limitations this paper aims to solve. First, the current approach was built to monitor single things (e.g., devices). However, as the complexity of nowadays IT infrastructure arises, means need to be enabled to monitor more than one thing using the introduced Situation Templates. Furthermore, currently, the STs are executed in a monolithic manner because in former scenarios, distribution was not necessary. In current approaches, e.g., involving Industrie 4.0, however, this is necessary. In this paper, we aim for enhancing our approach in order to be more fitting to recent scenarios.

III. Scenario and Requirements

In this section, we introduce a practical motivating scenario from the I4.0 domain, which is used throughout the paper to explain our approach. In the scenario, depicted in Figure 2, a specific part of the supply chain of a production company should be monitored. As depicted, there are several entities involved: (i) production machines, assembling products based on parts, and (ii) trucks, delivering the parts to be assembled. The monitoring should detect critical situations that could occur, for example, the failure of at least one of the machines, or a delivery delay of parts, e.g., caused by issues with

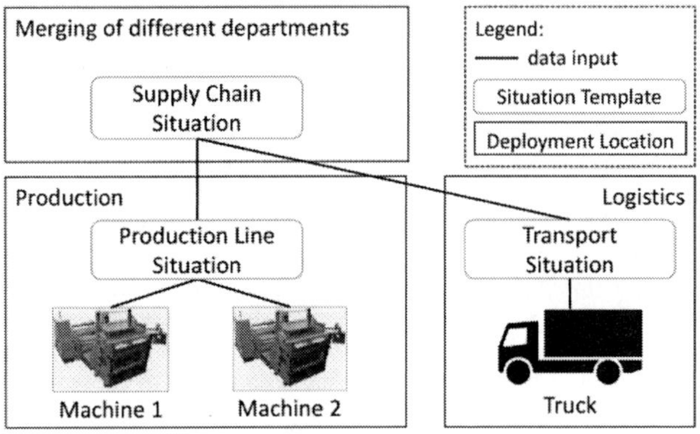

Figure 2. Motivating scenario for distributed situation recognition

trucks or with the supplier. Situations that could occur are: (i) *Production Line Situation*, indicating that one of the production machines is in an erroneous state, (ii) *Transport Situation*, indicating a problem with the truck, and (iii) *Supply Chain Situation*, indicating a problem with either the production line or the truck.

When applying our previous approach, described in Section II, to this scenario, new requirements arise that need to be coped with. We divide these requirements into ones that concern the modeling of STs and ones that concern the execution of the situation recognition. We derived 8 requirements R_1 to R_7 for this scenario.

Modeling Requirements
Three requirements focus on the modeling of the situation recognition using STs.

- R_1 - **More powerful Situation Templates:** With our previous approach (cf. Section II-B), single machines can be monitored in an efficient way as evaluated in [5], which was sufficient for previous scenarios. However, in recent scenarios involving Industry 4.0, the requirements are increasing. In our motivating scenario, it is important to model dependencies between multiple entities within a single ST, e.g., to recognize the *Production Line Situation*.
- R_2 - **Low modeling complexity:** In our previous approach, modeling STs involving a lot of context data has led to a cumbersome task and, consequently, to a high complexity and error-prone modeling. To cope with this issue, a new modeling approach is required that enables the reutilization of already existing STs to lower the modeling complexity of new STs.
- R_3 - **Domain-independence:** A consequence of the issue described in R_2 is domain-dependence. Large STs usually consist of a wide range of context data sources, e.g., Trucks or the Production Line of our scenario. However, these context data sources require domain experts of these specific areas. Consequently, STs need to be modeled by these experts together. This leads to high costs due to the communication overhead. Hence, our goal is to enable domain-independence for ST modeling.

Execution Requirements

- R_4 - **Low latency:** In many domains, latency plays a crucial role. Especially in Smart Factory environments, the industrial automation layer has strong requirements regarding end-to-end latency up to 1 ms or even lower [19]. Therefore, the execution of the situation recognition needs to adapt to those requirements, so that critical situations like machine failures can be recognized in a timely manner.
- R_5 - **Low network traffic:** In modern scenarios, large amounts of data are produced that need to be stored and processed in order to recognize situations. For example, an autonomous car produces about 35 GB/hour of data [20]. In comparison, Budomo et al. [21] conducted a drive test and recorded a maximum and minimum upload speed of 30Mbps (13.5 GB/hour) and 3.5Mbps (1.58 GB/hour), respectively, using the current mobile communication standard LTE-A. Therefore, transferring all data of an autonomous car to the cloud is currently impossible. Consequently, reducing the network traffic is an important issue when recognizing situations.
- R_6 - **Data security & privacy:** Especially the processing of company data needs to be secure and, furthermore, privacy needs to be ensured. However, especially when processing data in the Public Cloud, companies need to trust the Cloud providers that they provide the security they require. Alternatively, companies can keep their data close, i.e., in a trusted environment.
- R_7 - **Cross-company situation recognition:** Modern products and its components are rarely built completely by one company. Therefore, most actual scenarios are very complex, involve multiple companies, and require a cross-company situation recognition. Our motivating scenario in Figure 2 can be regarded as such an example, in which a manufacturing company cooperates with a logistics company. For example, a delayed delivery caused by a failure of the truck must be communicated to the manufacturing company. Consequently, our situation recognition approach needs to enable a cross-company situation recognition.

IV. Distribution of Situation Recognition

In our previous work, we already solved challenges regarding sensor registration and management [22], efficient solutions for a situation recognition [17], and the management of recognized situation [18]. Now, we concentrate on extending our previous approach by introducing a distribution of the situation recognition to fulfill the above-mentioned requirements R_1-R_7. For this, we first present (i) the modeling improvements for our approach to support the distribution we aim for. On this basis, we present (ii) the execution improvements to enable the distribution based on three distribution patterns including a decision support for each of those patterns.

The distributed situation recognition was implemented based on the existing prototype of our previous work, introduced in [17][18] by following adaptations: (i) the modeling for STs was extended, (ii) the transformation was enhanced to accept multiple things, and (iii) the communication between the distributed locations is enabled by messaging systems.

A. Modeling Improvements

In the following, we present the improvements regarding the modeling of STs to fulfill the requirements R_1-R_3. The extension of the STs, i.e. its schema, comprises (i) the modeling of multiple things within a single ST, and (ii) a layered modeling by reutilizing already modeled STs. These extensions are depicted in Figure 3. Requirement R_1 describes the need for the modeling of more powerful situations, e.g., *Production Line critical*. However, a production line itself does not contain any sensors but rather describes the coherence and arrangement of multiple machines. Therefore, to model a situation describing the production line, we need to model all machines of the production line into a single ST. By extending the Situation Template Schema to allow the modeling of multiple things, therefore, we fulfill requirement R_1.

It is obvious that from a certain amount of things in a single ST and each thing having multiple sensors, the complexity of modeling such a ST is becoming a problem. An excessive complexity restricts the usability of our modeling approach, hence, the reduction of the modeling complexity is required (cf. R_2). To cope with the increasing complexity of STs, we introduce the layered modeling approach. Instead of modeling everything within a single ST, we use situations as context input for further situation recognition. Thereby, we implicitly reuse already modeled STs. These situations can be divided into three classes: *local situations*, *hybrid situations*, and *global situations*. This classification is based on the context input of the respective situations and describes the hierarchy of situations. Local situations only receive context input by one or multiple things. Hybrid situations receive at least one local situation as input and context input of at least one thing. Global situations receive at least two situations, local or/and hybrid, as input. An equivalent modeling of the situation *Production Line critical* using the layered modeling approach is shown in Figure 3 (right side). Based on this comparison, we show the benefits of this approach:

- **Reusability:** By using situations as input, we reutilize existing STs. When modeling a global situation, we only need to model the relation between the already modeled local/hybrid situations similar to putting together building blocks. A further advantage is that the local/hybrid STs possibly were already used and tested for correctness, which lowers the error-proneness for modeling global situations.
- **Reduce complexity:** The reusability directly leads to less complex STs, since the modeling is based on the Divide and Conquer paradigm. By using the layered modeling approach, we fulfill the requirement R_2.
- **Distribution:** Since we do not have one single and complex ST, but instead, multiple smaller ones, we already have a beneficial starting point for the distribution of the situation recognition as we can simply execute the different STs at different locations.
- **Support for specific domains:** Having multiple things within a single ST could lead to the problem that knowledge from different domains is required. For example, motivating scenario contains three domains - manufacturing, logistics and their dependencies. Using the layered modeling approach, different domains can model STs independently. Requirement R_3 is fulfilled.

As a result, by introducing an extended Situation Template Schema to enable the modeling of multiple things within a single ST and the layered modeling approach, we fulfill all modeling requirements R_1-R_3.

B. Execution Improvements

The modeling improvements we presented in the last section serve as the foundation for the distribution of the situation recognition. As mentioned above, in our previous approach, the situation recognition was executed centralized in the cloud. Hence, all context data was sent to this cloud and was used as input for the situation recognition. However, lately, the term *Edge Computing* gains more and more attention. Shi et al. [6] define *the edge* as *"any computing and network resources along the path between data sources and cloud data centers"*. Therefore, in our context, Edge Computing refers to the processing of context data close to the data sources.

By introducing Edge Computing to our approach, a distribution of the situation recognition to the cloud and the edge can be performed. In the scenario of Figure 2, the distribution of the situation recognition seems obvious. Using the layered modeling approach, we can model the local situations *Production Line Situation* and *Transport Situation* and the global situation *Supply Chain Situation*. The situation recognition for the local situation is executed at the edge, i.e., locally in the factory or truck, respectively. The global situation is executed in the cloud and receives the local situations as input. However, based on the execution requirements R_4-R_7, this distribution might not always be ideal.

Therefore, in the following, we present the execution improvements resulting from the distribution of the situation recognition. First, we present the concept of context stripping and its benefits. Afterwards, we introduce three distribution patterns and a decision support for choosing the most suitable distribution pattern for a certain scenario.

1) Context Stripping: As presented in Section II-B, when a situation recognition is executed, situation objects are created that are defined by the Situation Model [18]. This situation object contains all context data that were used for the evaluation of this specific situation. In [18], we approximated the data volume of situation objects based on the amount of used context data. The results showed that the appended context data presents the majority of the data size of a situation object. Now, when using the layered modeling approach, we may use local situations that we recognized at the edge as input for the recognition of global situations in the cloud. That causes us to send all context data to the cloud again within the situation object. However, based on the scenario, we might not be interested in the context data of a situation object but only if the local situation occurred or not, so we can evaluate the global situation. Therefore, we introduce the concept of *context stripping*. By using context stripping, the context used for the situation recognition is not sent within the situation object. It only contains the most vital data for a further situation recognition in the cloud. Therefore, content-wise, a local situation only contains a boolean value, which describes if the local situation occurred or not and the required meta data for further processing.

This leads to a trade-off the user has to decide based on his requirements. By using context stripping, the data size of a situation object can be strongly reduced. However, the context

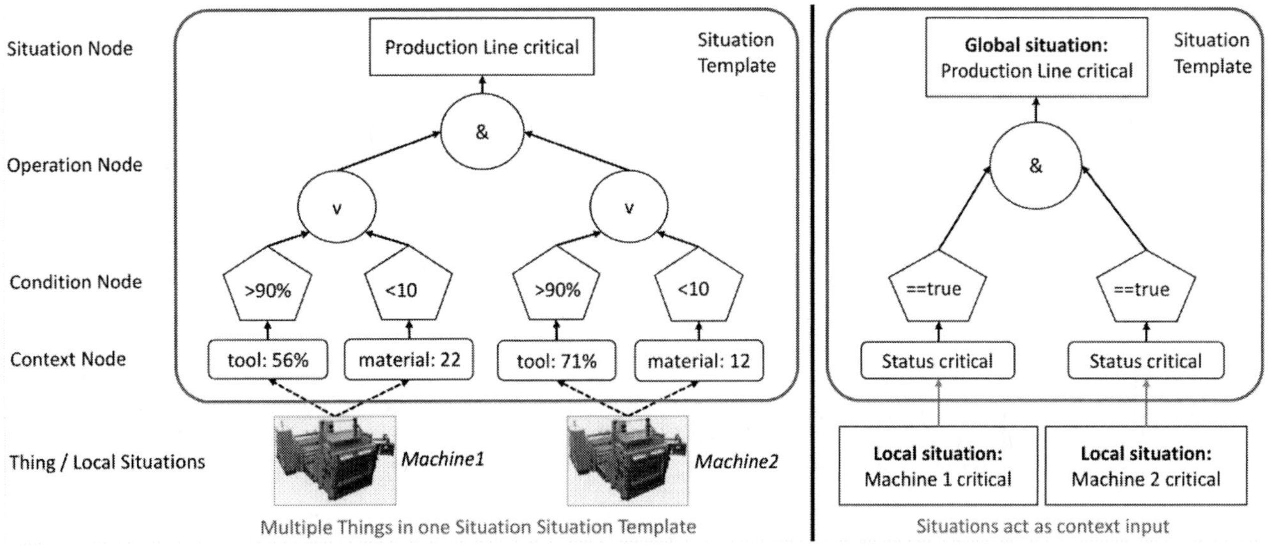

Figure 3. Modeling improvements for STs (legend see Figure 4)

data that led to the evaluation of a specific situation object is discarded after processing. In our first approach, we explicitly wanted to store the context data within situation objects for a detailed historization of situations. This historization, for example, can be used afterwards for a root cause analysis of detected situations based on the involved context data.

2) Distribution Patterns: As mentioned above, the distribution of the situation recognition is dependent on the execution requirements R_4-R_7. Therefore, a general solution for the distribution of the situation recognition is not possible. Instead, we introduce three different distribution patterns, depicted in Figure 4 based on the scenario shown in Figure 2. The *Type I* distribution pattern describes our previous approach. All context data, i.e., in this scenario, context data from a truck and two machines, is sent to the cloud. The situation recognition is executed in the cloud and all context data is available. In contrast, the *Type II* pattern describes the execution of the situation recognition at the edge, close to the data sources. In this case, it is often impossible to gather all context data from all sources, e.g., from the truck, since it is not part of the local network of the factory, where the machines are located. Therefore, only parts of the situation recognition may be executed at the edge. The *Type III* pattern is a hybrid solution based on both the *Type I* and *Type II* pattern and enables the execution of situation recognition at the edge, which results in local situations (i.e., *Production Line* and *Transport*) and the execution of situation recognition in the cloud, where the local situations are used to evaluate the global situation.

In the following, the different distribution patterns are described in more detail with regard to the execution requirements R_4-R_7. Each pattern comprises advantages for certain use cases and might not fulfill every execution requirement. Additionally, the presented distribution patterns are applicable to the distribution of data processing in general.

3) Type-I: Cloud-only (Figure 4, left): Despite many advantages of Edge Computing, the Type-I distribution pattern still is a viable option. Introducing Edge Computing is no trivial task and comprises multiple challenges [6]. Companies with low IT experience or no IT department benefit from outsourcing IT infrastructure and expertise to third-party cloud providers. This oftentimes is the case for SMEs, which then can solely focus on their products and the pay-as-you-go model provides a cost-effective and scalable infrastructure.

- R_4 - **Low latency:** Currently, when using an off-premise cloud, the requirement of 1 ms is already violated by the network latency itself. Therefore, requirement R_4 cannot be fulfilled.
- R_5 - **Low network traffic:** Since all context data must be sent to the cloud first, network traffic cannot be reduced. Requirement R_5 is not fulfilled.
- R_6 - **Data security & privacy:** Since all context data is sent to the cloud, new security risks are introduced. Furthermore, company policies might prohibit sending sensitive or personal context data to the cloud. Therefore, requirement R_6 is not fulfilled.
- R_7 - **Cross company situation recognition:** Since all data is available in the cloud, companies can work together to execute a collaborative situation recognition. Requirement R_7 is fulfilled.

As shown, the Type-I pattern does not fulfill most requirements. Still, in non-critical scenarios where high latency is acceptable, the network traffic is low or fluctuating and the data is allowed to be sent to the cloud by the companies' policies or government regulations, the Type-I pattern is a sensible option.

4) Type-II: Edge-only (Figure 4, middle): In comparison, the Type-II distribution pattern describes the execution of the whole situation recognition at the edge. As already mentioned, this is only possible if all context data is available at the edge. Therefore, the situation recognition of local situations is best-suited for an edge-only execution.

- R_4 - **Low latency:** Yi et al. [23] show that latency can be reduced by 82% by moving an application to the edge of the network. As the situation recognition is

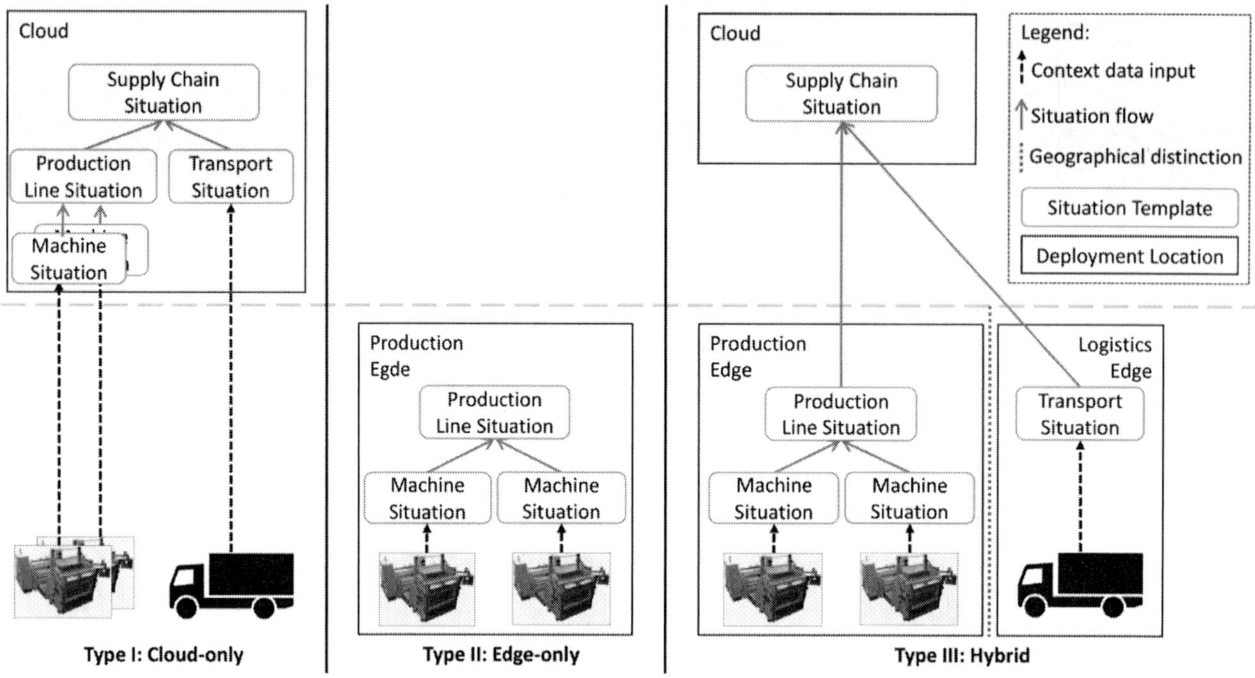

Figure 4. Distribution patterns

executed as close as possible to the data sources the requirement R_4 is fulfilled. With an execution time of 3ms for our situation recognition [17], the overall latency is kept comparably low.

- R_5 - **Low network traffic:** No context data is sent to the cloud, therefore, network traffic stays low and requirement R_5 is fulfilled.
- R_6 - **Data security & privacy:** One of the main concerns regarding the adoption of Cloud Computing still is security, especially in companies with few experience with Cloud Computing. Security and privacy of data is increased, since all context data and situations remain at the edge, i.e., a local network controlled by its company. Requirement R_6 is fulfilled.
- R_7 - **Cross company situation recognition:** In general, the data sources of different companies are geographically distributed and not in the same local network. Therefore, a cross company situation recognition is not possible. Requirement R_7 is not fulfilled.

Most requirements are fulfilled. However, more complex scenarios (cf. Figure 2) cannot be mapped to this pattern because of geographically distributed data sources. Therefore, the Type-II distribution pattern is best suited for company-internal situation recognition that fulfills critical requirements like latency and security. Especially in mobile environments, e.g., an autonomous truck, with high-volume data the Type-II pattern is a good option.

5) Type-III: Hybrid (Figure 4, right): Neither a Type-I nor a Type-II distribution pattern presents a viable option for our motivating scenario, since the truck produces too much data for a cloud-only solution and the geographical distribution of the data sources prevents an edge-only solution. Therefore, in the Type-III distribution pattern, the situation recognition is distributed to both the cloud and the edge. This leads to the recognition of local situations at the edge and global situations in the cloud and their advantages.

- R_4 - **Low latency:** The latency for local situations is reduced as described in Type-II. However, global situations are evaluated in the cloud and the latency is as described in Type-I. Therefore, the requirement R_4 is fulfilled only for local situations.
- R_5 - **Low network traffic:** As in Type-II, network traffic can be saved by shifting the situation recognition to the edge. The situation objects of the local situations must be sent to the cloud for the evaluation of global situations, thereby increasing network traffic. However, by using context stripping, the data size of situation objects can be massively reduced and still enable further processing of global situations. Therefore, requirement R_5 is fulfilled.
- R_6 - **Data security & privacy:** Security and privacy of local situations match the Type-II pattern. Again, when using context stripping for local situations, we support complex scenarios and do not have to send sensitive context data within situation objects to the cloud. Therefore, R_6 is fulfilled.
- R_7 - **Cross company situation recognition:** As in the Type-I distribution pattern, a collaborative situation recognition is possible. However, a big advantage is gained by using context stripping. Possibly sensitive context data of each company remains at their respective edge. Only context-stripped local situations are sent to the cloud for the collaborative evaluation of the global situation. Therefore, requirement R_8 is fulfilled.

TABLE I. FULFILLMENT OF EXECUTION REQUIREMENTS BY THE DISTRIBUTION PATTERNS

	R_4	R_5	R_6	R_7
Type-I: Cloud-only	X	X	X	✓
Type-II: Edge-only	✓	✓	✓	X
Type-III: Hybrid	✓	✓	✓	✓

Except reducing the latency for the evaluation of global situations, all requirements are fulfilled by this hybrid approach. Especially the usage of context stripping presents multiple advantages when transferring local situations to the cloud. The Type-III distribution pattern is best-suited for complex scenarios with multiple data sources that require a fast reaction to local situations and a centralized situation recognition of global situations without increasing the network traffic. Multiple companies can collaborate without sharing sensitive data or infringing government regulation.

Table I summarizes the analysis of the different distribution patterns. As shown, the Type-III hybrid approach fulfills all execution requirements.

V. SUMMARY AND FUTURE WORK

In this paper, we present an approach for distributed situation recognition. To support the distribution, we extend the Situation Template Schema so that multiple things and situations can be used for context input using a layered modeling approach. Furthermore, we present the concept of context stripping to reduce network traffic by removing the associated context of situation objects. We examine three distribution patterns based on execution requirements that are important for a situation recognition in complex environments.

In future work, we intend to create a sophisticated cost model, since choosing a suitable distribution pattern is very use-case dependent. This way, users can receive a more detailed decision support based on their specific properties and requirements, which can lead to a faster adoption of new technologies like Edge Computing.

Acknowledgment This work is partially funded by the BMWi project IC4F (01MA17008G).

REFERENCES

[1] D. Lucke, C. Constantinescu, and E. Westkämper, Manufacturing Systems and Technologies for the New Frontier: The 41st CIRP Conference on Manufacturing Systems May 26–28, 2008, Tokyo, Japan. London: Springer London, 2008, ch. Smart Factory - A Step towards the Next Generation of Manufacturing, pp. 115–118.

[2] L. Atzori, A. Iera, and G. Morabito, "The internet of things: A survey," Computer Networks, vol. 54, no. 15, 2010, pp. 2787 – 2805.

[3] J. S. He, S. Ji, and P. O. Bobbie, "Internet of things (iot)-based learning framework to facilitate stem undergraduate education," in Proceedings of the SouthEast Conference. ACM, 2017, pp. 88–94.

[4] M. Wieland, H. Schwarz, U. Breitenbücher, and F. Leymann, "Towards situation-aware adaptive workflows: SitOPT – A general purpose situation-aware workflow management system," in Pervasive Computing and Communication Workshops (PerCom Workshops). IEEE, 2015, pp. 32–37.

[5] P. Hirmer, M. Wieland, H. Schwarz, B. Mitschang, U. Breitenbücher, S. G. Sáez, and F. Leymann, "Situation recognition and handling based on executing situation templates and situation-aware workflows," Computing, 10 2016, pp. 1–19.

[6] W. Shi, J. Cao, Q. Zhang, Y. Li, and L. Xu, "Edge computing: Vision and challenges," IEEE Internet of Things Journal, vol. 3, no. 5, 2016, pp. 637–646.

[7] K. Häussermann, C. Hubig, P. Levi, F. Leymann, O. Simoneit, M. Wieland, and O. Zweigle, "Understanding and designing situation-aware mobile and ubiquitous computing systems," in Proc. of intern. Conf. on Mobile, Ubiquitous and Pervasive Computing. Citeseer, 2010, pp. 329–339.

[8] Q. Fang, Y. Zhao, G. Yang, and W. Zheng, Scalable Distributed Ontology Reasoning Using DHT-Based Partitioning. Springer Berlin Heidelberg, 2008, pp. 91–105.

[9] X. Wang, D. Q. Zhang, T. Gu, and H. Pung, "Ontology based context modeling and reasoning using OWL," in Pervasive Computing and Communications Workshops, 2004. Proceedings of the Second IEEE Annual Conference on, 2004.

[10] W. Dargie, J. Mendez, C. Mobius, K. Rybina, V. Thost, A.-Y. Turhan et al., "Situation recognition for service management systems using OWL 2 reasoners," in Pervasive Computing and Communications Workshops (PERCOM Workshops), 2013 IEEE International Conference on. IEEE, 2013, pp. 31–36.

[11] J. Attard, S. Scerri, I. Rivera, and S. Handschuh, "Ontology-based situation recognition for context-aware systems," in Proceedings of the 9th International Conference on Semantic Systems. ACM, 2013, pp. 113–120.

[12] B. Schilling, B. Koldehofe, U. Pletat, and K. Rothermel, "Distributed heterogeneous event processing: Enhancing scalability and interoperability of cep in an industrial context," in Proceedings of the Fourth ACM International Conference on Distributed Event-Based Systems. ACM, 2010, pp. 150–159.

[13] N. P. Schultz-Møller, M. Migliavacca, and P. Pietzuch, "Distributed complex event processing with query rewriting," in Proceedings of the Third ACM International Conference on Distributed Event-Based Systems, ser. DEBS '09. New York, NY, USA: ACM, 2009, pp. 4:1–4:12. [Online]. Available: http://doi.acm.org/10.1145/1619258.1619264

[14] K. V. Laerhoven and H. W. Gellersen, "Spine versus porcupine: a study in distributed wearable activity recognition," in Eighth International Symposium on Wearable Computers, vol. 1, Oct 2004, pp. 142–149.

[15] A. K. Dey, "Understanding and using context," Personal and ubiquitous computing, vol. 5, no. 1, 2001, pp. 4–7.

[16] P. Hirmer, M. Wieland, H. Schwarz, B. Mitschang, U. Breitenbücher, and F. Leymann, "SitRS - A Situation Recognition Service based on Modeling and Executing Situation Templates," in Proceedings of the 9th Symposium and Summer School On Service-Oriented Computing, 2015, Konferenz-Beitrag, pp. 113–127.

[17] A. C. Franco da Silva, P. Hirmer, M. Wieland, and B. Mitschang, "SitRS XT-Towards Near Real Time Situation Recognition," Journal of Information and Data Management, 2016.

[18] M. Mormul, P. Hirmer, M. Wieland, and B. Mitschang, "Situation model as interface between situation recognition and situation-aware applications," Computer Science - Research and Development, November 2016, pp. 1–12.

[19] O. N. Yilmaz, Y.-P. E. Wang, N. A. Johansson, N. Brahmi, S. A. Ashraf, and J. Sachs, "Analysis of ultra-reliable and low-latency 5g communication for a factory automation use case," in Communication Workshop (ICCW), 2015 IEEE International Conference on. IEEE, 2015, pp. 1190–1195.

[20] O. Moll, A. Zalewski, S. Pillai, S. Madden, M. Stonebraker, and V. Gadepally, "Exploring big volume sensor data with vroom," Proceedings of the VLDB Endowment, vol. 10, no. 12, 2017.

[21] J. Budomo, I. Ahmad, D. Habibi, and E. Dines, "4g lte-a systems at vehicular speeds: Performance evaluation," in Information Networking (ICOIN), 2017 International Conference on. IEEE, 2017, pp. 321–326.

[22] P. Hirmer, M. Wieland, U. Breitenbücher, and B. Mitschang, "Automated Sensor Registration, Binding and Sensor Data Provisioning," in CAiSE Forum, 2016.

[23] S. Yi, Z. Hao, Z. Qin, and Q. Li, "Fog computing: Platform and applications," in Hot Topics in Web Systems and Technologies (HotWeb), 2015 Third IEEE Workshop on. IEEE, 2015, pp. 73–78.

All links were last followed on May 22.

The "Bottom-up Smart City": Filling the Gap Between Theory and Practice

Clémentine Schelings & Catherine Elsen
LUCID Lab for User Cognition & Innovative Design
University of Liège
Liège, Belgium
e-mail: clementine.schelings@uliege.be; catherine.elsen@uliege.be

Abstract—**This paper explores the relatively new phenomenon of citizen participation in the Smart City context. We present a case study comparative analysis of two participatory approaches implemented in two European Smart Cities. Each of those operational perspectives is studied in view of the theoretical concepts conveyed by the scientific state of the art, this way highlighting similarities and gaps between theory and practice. The results are focused on the various existing interpretations of the "citizen participation" and the "Smart City" definitions, and on the different selection processes applied in both cases to recruit the participating citizens. The article closes with a discussion about key elements to keep in mind when implementing a bottom-up participative approach in the context of a Smart City.**

Keywords-Smart City; citizen participation; Smart City definitions; operational perspective; selection of participants.

I. INTRODUCTION

The first Smart Cities were essentially focused on technological deployment aiming at optimizing urban performances, for instance thanks to freely accessible internet access, sensors and other pervasive devices. After this first wave of completely top-down and techno-centric cities (such as Songdo in South Korea or Masdar in the United Arab Emirates), we are slowly entering the era of a more bottom-up and participative model of Smart Cities. The citizens are now given an increasingly important role in the making of their smart built environments, because their acceptability is essential to insure the sustainability of the global smart model [1]. If many researchers acknowledge the fact that smart citizens are indeed key to Smart Cities, few information is yet available about how to implement a renewed participative approach, built on 1970 participatory models, in the making of such smart urban environments.

This research is one of the first steps of a larger research project, that is mainly focused on the citizens' perspective regarding the Smart City and the participative approach. This paper rather aims at studying and comparing different participatory initiatives conducted in Smart Cities particularly known for their citizen engagement and their bottom-up dynamics. The goal here is to document actual participative approaches in order to extract some key elements regarding citizen participation in the Smart City.

Comparing scientific perspectives with day-to-day, operational implementations of Smart City initiatives, this paper is structured in four more sections. In Section II, we present a short literature review about participation in the Smart City. Section III then describes the interview-based methodology used for the comparative analysis of participative processes implemented in two carefully selected Smart Cities (one in the United Kingdom, one in the Netherlands). Section IV describes the obtained results: Subsection A gives the participatory context, while Subsection B is focused on the practical vision of two key definitions (Smart City and citizen participation) compared to more theoretical ones coming from the literature review, Subsection C presents the participants' selection processes in both chosen cases. Section V discusses the results and raises some questions in regard of what both chosen Smart Cities consider as "best practices", given their specific contexts.

II. STATE OF THE ART

This state of the art is kept voluntary short and will only present major theoretical models underlying the concepts of Smart City and citizen participation. Our subsequent intention is indeed to further study literature review in regard of empirical results in order to establish a comparison between theoretical and operational perspectives.

Two main concepts are at the root of this research project, namely "Smart City" and "citizen participation". Both concepts carry a multitude of (sometimes confused) definitions as they designate multifaceted realities [2][3]. As far as the "Smart City" concept is concerned, there are indeed a multitude of definitions and no real consensus about the meaning of this "buzzword" [4]. Giffinger's definition, one of the most frequently referred to, dissects the concept into six axes: economy, environment, governance, living, mobility and people [5]. Especially because of this "people" component, the citizen participation has lately become more and more popular in the Smart City context [6][7], building on the realization that citizens' potential rejection of the Smart City concepts could entirely jeopardize the sustainability of the global smart model itself [4][8]. Citizens are thus considered as key actors of the making of the Smart City and their sensitization and participation are the first steps towards awareness and acceptability [2]. Gradually, the techno-centric smart environments give way to more eco-systemic Smart Cities and a shift is observed from the triple helix to the quadruple-helix model [9][10]. Side by side with universities, governments and industries, citizens are henceforth recognized as the fourth main stakeholder of the smart innovation [11]. Even though many authors nowadays share this viewpoint and promote citizens' engagement and empowerment, few information is available about how to concretely apply citizen participation to the context of Smart Cities [12]. Moreover, we suggest that older models of citizen participation, such as Arstein's ladder or Glass' objectives of participation [13][14], should be re-interpreted and might differently take place in practice given the opportunities offered by new technologies.

It is therefore crucial to confront theoretical and practical realities and to explore what local actors have in mind when referring to citizen participation in the Smart City.

III. METHODOLOGY

The methodology used to conduct this research is a comparative analysis of two cases, nurtured by semi-structured interviews with several stakeholders linked to smart projects and participative initiatives in each of those cases. This paper focuses on two European Smart Cities, one in the United Kingdom and the other one in the Netherlands. In both cities, one research lab was chosen because it meets the following criteria: it is localized in an internationally recognized Smart City, it works in collaboration with the city officials and its main research activities are linked to citizen participation in future urban environments. Beyond those similarities, the two research centers remain quite different in their approaches. The Dutch lab generally considers self-organized citizens' communities and bottom-up movements as essential triggers for any launched project, while the British lab rather tries to integrate a participative dimension to existing projects that would not make sense otherwise. Thus, the Dutch lab is always involved in participatory initiatives, but the British lab also conducts some research projects without any citizen participation. Another difference between the labs lies in the end-use of the material produced through the participative process. The British lab seeks to develop a marketable product, while the Dutch lab rather promotes open-access material that can be freely reused after the end of each project. A last difference is due to the various profiles and backgrounds of the members of the two labs that therefore develop different identities. The British lab is mainly composed of computer scientists using data for a socio-technological purpose. The Dutch lab brings together researchers with data, design and digital humanities backgrounds.

In practice, each interview was expected to last about one hour, but the effective length varies between forty and eighty minutes. Several types of stakeholders were interviewed: directors of the research centers, labs' team members, Smart City managers, city officials and other experts from the fields of participation, technology and urban planning. Given this variety of interviewees' profiles, different sets of questions were prepared, in line with the specific expertise of each actor. In addition, some essential issues were discussed with the complete sample of respondents, such as their own definitions of "Smart City" and "citizen participation".

As a first step of our comparative analysis, this paper will focus on only four interviews and more specifically on the results of meetings conducted with two lab directors and two team members. We decided to start our study with those stakeholders because they are very close to the realities on the ground: the team members are the day-to-day operational actors, while the directors are the spokespersons of each lab and therefore structure those labs' vision and attitude. The idea is to understand both global visions of those two labs and to compare their different interpretation of the participative approach, given their actual perception of the Smart City.

Globally, eight main themes are addressed through the interviews (see Table 1). Additional questions regarding the presentation of the city (specificities, history, population) and the policy (objectives, priorities, citizens' input) are discussed with city officials and Smart City managers, but won't be presented in this paper.

IV. RESULTS

The results of the four interviews are structured in three subsections. First, we will present the contexts in which citizens become active participants for both cities. Then, we will present interviewees' definitions of the Smart City and the citizen participation, in comparison with the scientific state of the art. Eventually, we will compare the participants' selection processes as conducted in both labs and we will study the impact such processes have on the recruited citizens' profiles.

A. Participatory context

The citizen participation is a complex process that may tire the citizens if their input is repeatedly requested for each and every project related to the Smart City. Therefore, it is of crucial importance to wisely choose topics for which participants' contribution is considered essential. Both labs have a different strategy regarding this issue. The British lab focuses on "*the stress points in the city (...), priorities, which have been identified with the council*" and uses citizen participation mainly to get feedbacks about the solutions developed by the researchers in cooperation with the local authorities. The logic of the Dutch lab is quite different. Once again, they start from context-specific urban problems, but the chosen topics result from shared interests between the citizens' preoccupations and the local authorities' priorities. Thus citizens are always involved in projects that they feel

TABLE I. MAIN THEMES STRUCTURING THE INTERVIEWS WITH THE DIRECTORS AND THE TEAM MEMBERS OF THE LAB

Common themes	Directors
- Presentation of each actor (background and role) - Own definitions of the two main concepts (Smart City and citizen participation) - Presentation of concrete projects (context, success stories, possible improvements) - Participatory approach (benefits, drawbacks, challenges) - Technology (role, ethics, privacy)	- Contacts with other stakeholders of the ecosystem (city officials, citizens, industrial partners) **Team members** - Participatory methodology (phases, methods, objectives) - Participants (roles, selection criteria, profiles)

concerned about, and that they wanted to integrate even prior to any involvement from the city itself. Another difference between the two approaches is that British citizens often participate at the end of the process, while the Dutch citizens always participate from the beginning and generally during the whole project.

B. Definitions

The two following subsections aim to define the Smart City and the citizen participation on basis of the interpretations proposed by the four interviewees. The results are examined with respect to the state of the art, highlighting the convergences and the divergences between theory and practice.

1) Smart City: This section focuses on the definition of the Smart City, as perceived by the stakeholders interviewed on the ground. On the basis of the most widespread definitions, we will compare the different visions hold by those experts (see Table 2 and Table 3).

The first interesting observation is that there is a distinction between their current vision (see Table 2) and their prospective vision (see Table 3) of what the Smart City is. In other words, the interviewees are fully conscious that the Smart City is an ongoing process that can be described on the one hand on the basis of current initiatives, with their promising achievements and their manifest limitations, or,

TABLE II. INTERVIEWEES' CURRENT VISION OF THE SMART CITY

The Smart City is...		Smart City	
		United-Kingdom	*Netherlands*
Interviewees	***Directors of the labs***	DU1 a technology-connoted word DU2 a city for one citizen category	DN1 a set of fully autonomous systems DN2 a top-down controlled city DN3 an easily managed city DN4 a city of "*dumb citizens*"
	Team members	MU1 a smartphone-adapted city MU2 a fuzzy concept	MN1 a set of technological infrastructures MN2 a product of big technology companies MN3 a concept disconnected from citizens MN4 an optimized and efficient city

TABLE III. INTERVIEWEES' PROSPECTIVE VISION OF THE SMART CITY

Smart City should be ...		Smart City	
		United-Kingdom	*Netherlands*
Interviewees	***Directors of the labs***	DU3 a technology-improved city DU4 an inclusive city	DN5 a less obvious city management DN6 a city of creative citizens DN7 a city of "*smart citizens that are able to fulfill their own information needs*"
	Team members	MU3 a set of facilitating technologies MU4 a support in daily life MU5 an assistance for everybody	MN5 /

DU = Director of the lab in the United-Kingdom (UK); DN = Director of the lab in the Netherlands; MU = team Member of the lab in the UK; MN = team Member of the lab in the Netherlands

on the other hand, on the basis of the likely evolutions and hopes for the future.

In the interviewees' discourses, we obviously find key elements that meet some definitions from the state of the art. The interviewees' propositions are identified by codes (see Table 2 and Table 3), which are referenced in brackets hereafter.

First of all, each expert mentions the technological aspect of the Smart City, be it considered as a positive or a negative element (DU1, DU3, MU1, MU3, DN1, MN1-2). Following some authors, new technologies are obviously part of the Smart City, in the sense that they support any other key aspect of the city such as wellbeing and quality of life [6][15]. This vision is shared by the interviewees, but perhaps in a more nuanced way as they feel that actual Smart Cities may misinterpret this use of technology, making it an end per se especially due the market pressure. However, the British team member still believes that technological developments will evolve into daily-life facilitators (MU3-4). The Dutch lab is more cautious and considers that the current practical message conveyed by the Smart City is not yet the perfect solution for our future urban ideal (MN5). Actually, this nuance is also the consequence of an almost exclusively top-down governance of many smart projects (DN2). This approach, although neglecting citizens' input (MN3), provides the advantage of easily managing the city (DN3, DN5) and rather efficiently optimizing its day-to-day operation [5][16]. Ben Letaifa yet emphasizes the importance of a complementary bottom-up approach through citizen participation [4]. Furthermore, Giffinger insists on the fact that a city cannot be smart and efficient (MN4) unless citizen's intelligence is valued and exploited [5]. According to the interviewees, citizens should indeed play a specific role in their smart urban environments, and they should be empowered in order to actively participate (DN4, DN6-7). The Dutch director even specifies that citizens should themselves be able to respond to their information needs, i.e., to become "*self-decisive, independent and aware citizens*" [5]. This citizen autonomy is only possible in an inclusive Smart City (DU2, DU4, MU5) and one of the next big challenges is to limit obstacles to such inclusion, such as the digital divide [17]. Finally, compared to the literature, one important aspect is missing from the interviewees' discourses: sustainability. Surprisingly, no participant refers to environmental and demographic issues while those are among the main reasons to promote smart initiatives, offering a long-term solution for our urban environments [18][19]. This demonstrates the extent to which the Smart City is a complex concept with many meanings and no unanimous definition, especially in regard of specific, locally constrained situations (MU2).

2) Citizen participation: Another notion difficult to grasp is the citizen participation, although this time it goes back to a nearly fifty-year-old concept [20]. Throughout the years, the participatory approach has evolved into new practices and its "smart" interpretation is certainly still another perspective to take into account. Based on the experts' interviews and the keywords they use, we identify four main axes around which we summarize their propositions in order to characterize participation in the age of Smart Cities: communication, citizen control, conditions and data manipulation (Figure 1).

The two labs generally tend to agree on some key aspects of citizen participation, but they both insist on different axes. First of all, the British lab notices that participation is above all **communication**, and most preferably two-way communication. Information has to be exchanged between citizens and power holders, be they researchers or local authorities, because every actor's perspective is valuable and should at least be listened to. There are several levels of communication depending on the contribution of the participants, who can either just receive information, propose their own ideas or even negotiate with the power holders. British Lab's actors put a certain emphasis on verbal exchanges, which do not yet suffice to qualify as participation according to some authors [21]. One step further, both labs agree with Arnstein and consider that "*citizen participation is citizen power*", meaning that citizens should have a real impact on the decision-making of any participative process [13]. Citizens are not just informed, educated or consulted to ease tensions, but should have an actual voice translated into action [13][22]. The Dutch lab considers that this **citizen control** goes hand in hand with involved and empowered citizens, which means that they are given the opportunity to actively and wisely participate. Furthermore, anybody should enjoy such opportunity, according to both labs, irrespective of gender, social status or even technology acquaintance. Beyond

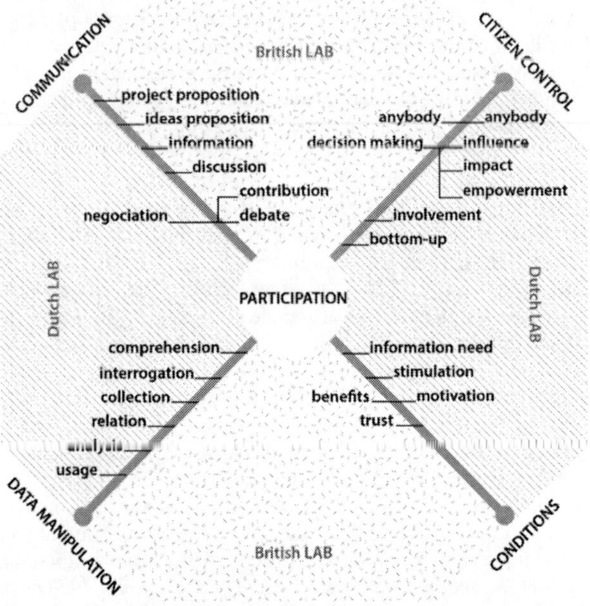

Figure 1. Axes of citizen participation on basis of interviewees' visions

being offered with the possibility to participate, both labs are conscious that citizens' willingness to participate is crucial and that they are some **conditions** that can ease the participative process and impact its implementation. The Dutch lab, in accordance with Klandermans and Oegema, specifies that the participants have to be motivated in order to actually take part to the project [23]. More importantly, participation often arises from an information need, directly expressed by the participants or identified after a stimulation phase. Consequently, citizens should be present from the early phases of the project [24], in order to make sure their needs will nurture the project definition. Moreover, the British lab is convinced that participation cannot efficiently operate without trust and benefits. Citizens are indeed more prone to participate if they "*foresee the benefits in the long run*", such as time and money savings. Finally, the fourth axis concerns **data manipulation**, which is intrinsically linked to the era of the Smart Cities. This axis has yet not been extensively documented in the literature review about citizen participation, maybe because there is a temporal gap between participatory theories introduced in the 70s and the first references to smart technologies appearing in the early 2000s. The "data manipulation" designates the way citizens interact with the data produced through the participative process. According to the Dutch lab, citizen participation is not limited to data collection, but should extend to their understanding, appropriation (interrogation and relation), analysis and usage by the citizens in order to create new knowledge. Indeed, new technologies might impact participative processes and are seen as an empowering factor, since "*digital technology allows cities to engage with citizens in decision-making processes*" [7].

C. *Selection of participants*

Given their different approaches, the two labs also show some discrepancies regarding the participants' selection. This section will present which participant profiles are targeted when a participative process is implemented, according to each Smart City. One recurrent goal in participatory processes is to make everyone participate, but in practice it is considered as nearly impossible. To select the participants, both labs therefore start from a local neighborhood, but their different interpretation of "local" has implications on the profiles of the sampled participants. Figure 2 summarizes the descriptions proposed by the two labs regarding recurrent citizen profiles taking part to their smart initiatives. The two shaded zones in Figure 2 highlight the keywords discribing similar citizens' profiles in both labs.

The Dutch lab "*select(s) (...) citizens basically by tapping into existing platforms or organizations that feed into the community*" while the British lab focuses on one specific geographical area. As a matter of fact, the Dutch interpretation is linked to existing communities that have already initiated some projects in order to solve local issues. In line with its research interests, the Dutch lab chooses to support and develop the ideas of the community, because it

Figure 2. Participants' profiles on basis of interviewees' selection process

seems more relevant to tackle actual people's concerns and to meet a real need. The British perspective is quite different and rather aims at testing on pilot sites some technologies, that would in fine be deployed at scale, requiring to get more "*general users*". Therefore, the British researchers just select a neighborhood and consequently the whole group of people living there. Given this divergent selection criterion, participants present different profiles in both samples. As far as the Dutch community members are concerned, they are of course very active and are described as "*involved*" and "*invested*" in the topic or even in concrete actions. This also means more environmental-conscious citizens that are generally interested in any initiative related to the smart city agenda. Since the British recruitment is made on a voluntary basis, the same super-enthusiastic profiles are also present but this time they are not self-organized around common values. The only condition to participate to the British project is to be equipped, i.e., for instance in a project of garden watering the condition is to have a garden. Besides the always-involved people, other profiles show up such as careless people, technology- and green-reluctant citizens that may decide to participate in order to save time or money for instance. Contrary to the Dutch communities, the British participants therefore constitute a less homogeneous sample presenting a limited amount of shared values and interests, but rather a group of people motivated to participate for various reasons.

V. Discussion

The participative approach is gaining more and more popularity in Smart City projects, but there is very little practical advice about how to conduct a participatory methodology in such specific context. Given the ground experience of the interviewed experts, we identify several questions emerging from their ongoing and completed projects in terms of concept definitions and selection of participants. Those key elements provide useful information both for scientific researchers and operational stakeholders.

First, the various existing interpretations of the Smart City concept definitely have an impact on its operational implementation. For instance, the concept of pervasive technology seems to play a major part in the current vision of the Smart City, but the citizen is expected to play a larger role in our future smart cities. The interviewees' prospective vision of the Smart City is generally closer to the definitions found in the scientific state of the art, while their current vision is less optimistic and is probably nurtured by the first failures encountered by Smart City projects around the world. Moreover, this variety of interpretations is linked to the fact that "*the smart city concept encompasses intangible aspects such quality of life and well-being components, whose measurement is subjective and difficult to perform*" [25]. Given the plethora of definitions, each ecosystem of actors working on smart initiatives should at least, and as a priority, agree on a shared vision, generating clear objectives and means to achieve them. The question to keep in mind is: how do we define the Smart City, and especially regarding the roles played by the technologies and by the citizens?

The second attention point concerns the definition of the citizen participation. Among the four axes previously identified (Figure 1), the communication, the citizen control and the conditions are explicitly discussed in the literature review, but the data manipulation is not yet part of the traditional scientific discourse. Citizen appropriation of the produced data is nonetheless a new form of participation and this technological dimension is even more crucial in the current smart context. This late integration of this data component as an additional facet of the citizen participation is clue that older concepts introduced in the 70s should evolve and that new participatory tools and methods are necessary to complement the existing ones. Therefore, one question to ask is: how can the new technologies support the participative process and the citizens' active, inclusive involvement? Furthermore, the interviewees' interpretations about citizen participation introduce the notion of citizens' motivation, nurturing our third focus point.

The results regarding the selection of the citizens show that participants can be characterized by different motivation spectrums: Dutch citizens share the same values while the British participants have more diverse interests. Following Deci, the participants' motivation may have intrinsic or extrinsic sources [26]. In other words, the citizens can respectively decide to participate "*because it is inherently interesting or enjoyable*" or "*because it leads to a separable outcome*" like for instance a reward [26]. In our case, the benefits promoted by the British lab, such as technology exclusivity, time or money savings, might be identified as extrinsic motivations. The Dutch participants rather seem to be motivated by intrinsic factors, such as the personal willingness to take part to the life of their community. According to Amabile's extensive research on the subject, this dichotomy between extrinsic and intrinsic motivations has consequences on the participants' creativity: extrinsic motivations could undermine the intrinsic motivation and the creative outputs, because the subject is not performing for its own sake anymore but rather for an external purpose [27]. Therefore, in our opinion, extrinsically motivated people will maybe more easily grow weary than intrinsically motivated citizens, who will probably commit themselves to participate in the long run. Consequently, our third question is: what are the citizens' motivations and what is the potential impact on the participants' long-term involvement within the project?

Another important consequence regarding the participants' selection of the participants is related to the representativeness of the sample. One recurrent wish of the interviewees is to reach everybody, but they agree that this dream scenario is too optimistic. Therefore, the two labs developed their own practical approach. On the one hand, the Dutch lab relies on existing communities, already active and probably prone to participate. On the other hand, the British lab recruits the most motivated citizens from a limited geographical area, based on some kind of "*first come, first served*" rule. The British lab then hopes to get more "*general users*" in the sense that the researchers do not know anything about the selected citizens, nor about their diverse motivations, leaving the possibility to include participants who have reservations about some aspects of the project. Even if the British sample is more heterogeneous, none of the two labs insures a representative sample. We should then be aware that each approach provides different target audiences and ask ourselves: how will the participants be selected and what are the consequences on the variety of the citizen profiles and, as a result, on the project outcomes?

VI. Conclusion and Future Work

This paper considers the citizen participation in the Smart City from the operational perspective. Based on interviews with ground actors, two Smart Cities' perceptions and participative approaches are compared and confronted with the literature review. The results show that the theoretical definitions of the "Smart City" rather correspond to the interviewees' prospective visions, while their current vision is not that optimistic, especially regarding the role played by the citizens. The interviewees' interpretation of the "citizen participation" is close to the existing theoretical models, but enriched by a new dimension related to the technological era, that we call "data manipulation". Regarding the participants' selection, striving to reach every citizen is seen as an un-achievable ideal and both labs develop their own alternative approach, tapping into existing communities or focusing on a specific geographical area. This choice has a direct impact on the participants' profiles, in terms of interests and motivations, or even creativity and commitment to the project. The nuanced interviewees' visions highlight key elements that should be kept in mind while implementing a participative approach in the Smart City. Given the variety of interpretations, further research will explore other case studies nurturing our comparative analysis. Future work will also focus on the citizens' perspective regarding their participation in the Smart City (preferences, barriers and motivations).

Acknowledgment

This research is part of the "Wal-e-Cities" project, funded by the FEDER and the Walloon region. The authors would like to thank the funding authorities, as well as all who contributed to this research, in particular the interviewed lab directors and team members.

References

[1] T. Monfaredzadeh and R. Krueger, "Investigating social factors of sustainability in a smart city," Procedia Engineering, vol. 118, pp. 1112-1118, 2015.

[2] M. Angelidou, "Smart city policies: a spatial approach," Cities, vol. 41, pp. S3-S11, 2014.

[3] K. Maier, "Citizen participation in planning: climbing a ladder?, " European Planning Studies, 9-6, pp. 707-719, 2001.

[4] S. Ben Letaifa, "How to strategize smart cities: revealing the SMART model," J. of Business Research, vol. 68, pp. 1414-1419, 2015.

[5] R. Giffinger et al., Smart cities: ranking of European medium-sized cities. Centre of Regional Science, Vienna University of Technology, 2007.

[6] R. G. Hollands, "Will the real smart city please stand up? Intelligent, progressive or entrepreneurial," City, vol. 12, no. 3, pp. 303-320, 2008.

[7] J. Willems, J. Van den Bergh, and S. Viaene, "Smart city projects and citizen participation: the case of London," in Public sector management in a globalized world, R. Andeßner, D. Greiling and R. Vogel, Eds. Wiesbaden: NPO-Management, Springer Gabler, pp. 249-266, 2017.

[8] A.-G. Paetz, E. Dütschke, and W. Fichtner, "Smart homes as a means to sustainable energy consumption: a study of consumer perceptions," Journal of Consumer Policy, vol. 35, pp. 23-41, 2012.

[9] L. Leydesdorff and M. Deakin, "The triple-helix model of smart cities: a neo-evolutionary perspective," Journal of Urban Technology, vol. 18, no. 2, pp. 53-63, 2011.

[10] R. P. Dameri, "Comparing smart and digital city: initiatives and strategies in Amsterdam and Genoa. Are they digital and/or smart?," in Smart City, R. P. Dameri and C. Rosenthal-Sabroux, Eds. Cham: Springer, pp. 45-88, 2014.

[11] D. Schuurman, B. Baccarne, L. De Marez, and P. Mechant, "Smart ideas for smart cities: investigating crowdsourcing for generating and selecting ideas for ICT innovation in a city context," Journal of Theoretical and Applied Electronic Commerce Research, vol. 7, no. 3, pp. 49-62, 2012.

[12] V. Thomas, D. Wang, L. Mullagh, and N. Dunn, "Where's Wally? In search of citizen perspectives on the smart city ," Sustainability, vol. 8, no. 3, pp. 207-219, 2016.

[13] S. R. Arnstein, "A ladder of citizen participation," J. of the American Institute of Planners, vol. 35-4, pp. 216-224, 1969.

[14] J. J. Glass, "Citizen participation in planning: the relationship between objectives and techniques," Journal of the American Institute of Planners, vol. 45, no. 2, pp. 180-189, 1979.

[15] R. P. Dameri, "Searching for smart city definition: a comprehensive proposal," International Journal of Computers & Technology, vol. 11, no. 5, pp. 2544-2551, 2013,

[16] S. P. Hall, "Creative cities and economic development," Urban Studies, vol. 37, no. 4, pp. 639-649, 2000.

[17] D. Gooch, A. Wolff, G. Kortuem, and R. Brown, "Reimagining the role of citizens in smart city projects," Adjunct Proc. of the 2015 ACM Int. Joint Conf. on Pervasive and Ubiquitous Computing, New York, 2015, pp. 1587-1594.

[18] A. Vanolo, "Is there anybody out there? The place and role of citizens in tomorrow's smart cities," Futures, vol. 82, pp. 26-36, 2016.

[19] H. Chourabi et al., "Understanding smart cities: an integrative framework," 45th Hawaii International Conference on System Sciences, HICSS, Maui, 2012, pp. 2289-2297.

[20] M.-H. Bacqué and M. Gauthier, "Participation, urban planning and urban studies," Participations, vol. 1, no. 1, pp. 36-66, 2011.

[21] R. Luck, "Dialogue in participatory design," Design studies, vol. 24, no. 6, pp. 523-535, 2003.

[22] R. Luck, "Learning to talk to users in participatory design situations," Design Studies, vol. 28, no. 3, pp. 217-242, 2007.

[23] B. Klandermans and D. Oegema, "Potentials, networks, motivations, and barriers: steps towards participation in social movements,", vol. 52, no. 4, pp. 519-531, 1987.

[24] G. Rowe and L. J. Frewer, "Public participation methods: a framework for evaluation," vol. 25, no. 1, pp. 3-29, 2000.

[25] R. Carli, M. Dotoli, R. Pellegrino, and L. Ranieri, "Measuring and managing the smartness of cities: a framework for classifying performance indicators," 2013 IEEE International Conference on Systems, Man, and Cybernetics (SMC), pp. 1288-1293, 2013.

[26] R. M. Ryan and E. L. Deci, "Intrinsic and extrinsic motivations: classic definitions and new directions," Contemporary Educ. Psychology, vol. 25, pp. 54-67, 2000.

[27] T. M. Amabile, "Social environments that kill creativity," in Readings in Innovation, S. S. Gryskiewiz and D. A. Hills, Eds. Greensboro, NC: Center for Creative Leadership, 1992.

Smart Learning Extended Environment: Connecting Anywhere People And Organizations

Piergiuseppe Ellerani
University of Salento
Lecce, Italy
email: piergiuseppe.ellerani@unisalento.it

Carlo Alberto Tenchini
Sharp Electronic Italia
Milano, Italy
email: carlo.tenchini@sharp.eu

Daniele Barca
Middle School "IC3 Mattarella"
Modena, Italy
email: daniele.barca@alice.it

Abstract— **The paper presents a case study aimed to realize a Smart Learning Environment, using an integration of technologies (digital environment, videoconference, new generation of interactive whiteboard) to sustain a Smart School. Data were collected with quantitative and qualitative method. Teachers and students are realizing a digital course for data base library school content.**

Keywords-smart school; whiteboard device; personal learning devices; videoconference.

I. Introduction. Smart Learning and Professional Development

The outcomes of international research on student learning [1][2] and teachers' practices and beliefs [3]-[5], have supported the debate on the need to raise the quality of schools. Nations policies have introduced reforms to better prepare students for the changed conditions of the 21st century [6].

The outcomes on the use of technologies show how the fundamental variable to increase the potential of learning is strictly related to transfer the student control over the learning process. Consequently, "how" people use technologies in learning contexts, becomes much more important than the technologies themselves. As Hattie demonstrated [3][7][8], the processes based on peer tutoring, the use of technologies to construct complex artifacts, or even the interaction organized by teaching methods, are those which better produce evidence learning.

Research on students' learning processes has led to highlight how:

- the principle that learning is not effectively a pure solitary activity, but it is a social action distributed in the context [7]; that the individual construction of knowledge takes place through processes of interaction, negotiation of meanings and cooperation with others [9]-[14]. Consequently, this perspective requires coherent methods of organizing and conducting the class [7];
- the principle of cognitive modification [15][16] is the result of a process of continuous interaction with artifacts, people and problems placed in the context, where the imitative processes [17][18] and "embodied" simulation [19][20] make evident new frontiers for more effective procedural and developmental learning (both cognitive and emotional) [21];
- the principle of inference of the environment/ context on learning allows to form "classes" competencies [10] such as creativity and innovation, problem solving and learning to learn [22]-[24]. The new media (and perhaps more significantly the web-based "social media") have a huge impact on the worldviews of individuals and groups; they also constitute forms of social belonging independent of geographic proximity [25].

Learning contexts are defined as inclusive of digital technologies [26]-[28] and are composed of a physical/spatial and digital dimension in which students realize their activities, even their tools, documents and other artifacts. In this sense technology can support deep learning in many ways, developing extensive learning contexts in which technologies are part of the process development. In particular it is shown how the interactive use of video is one of the forms that most involve deep learning. TALIS-OECD [3][4] contrarily shows a moderate percentage of teachers who orientate their practices in coherence with the research, through paths of exchange and cooperation with colleagues and the world of pedagogical reflection.

One aspect is therefore that teachers are involved in skills training: organizing learning and skills development, leading classes with more effective and innovative methodologies [10][29] in increasingly active learning environments; and engaging is therefore a perspective that requires the extension and dissemination of good practices widely spread.

The continuous training of teachers should therefore become a dynamic and transformative process of professional action, also modifying both the organization of schools - understood as a set of interdependent systems - and the forms of participation in the improvement of institutions, capable of modifying the adaptation matured, with a new update culture.

Scaffolding systems for continuous training thought as transformation and progress highlighted and sustained by research [30]-[34] can be an effective reference for innovation and quality of schools. It is therefore necessary to change the convictions rooted in teachers, expanding their repertoire of thought, perspectives, teaching methodologies; on the other hand to constantly develop and update a professional knowledge base on teaching and learning, starting from the research evidence, on the provisions of the adult mind, on the "in-action" connected research [29].

Hattie meta-analysis [7] also highlights some features of today's professional learning communities, increasingly considered an essential tool for establishing collaborative relationships and building capacity for change within the educational institution [35]-[38]. At the same time, professional learning communities become a way for schools to reduce isolation and learn together how to create sustainable change, while also measuring the achievement of improvement goals [35][37][39][40]. A professional learning community can be therefore defined as the set consisting of teachers, managers, administrative staff, staff, facilitators, researchers who share work to improve and progressively develop student learning [41]-[43]. It creates innovative, effective and powerful learning environments for the training of everyone's operations, to train empowerment and agency, to pursue personal, social and community goals.

The structure of the paper is following: in section 2 is described the concept of Smart School and the technology as devices. In section 3 we present the hypothesis, the research design and the people involved. In section 4 the activities designed and realized using devices to evaluate the case study. In section 5 we present some, and work-in progress, conclusions.

II. SMART LEARNING AND SCHOOLS

In order to ensure that learners are provided a relevant and engaging learning experience, it is becoming increasingly vital for such Smart Learning Environments (SLE) to be implemented in secondary and tertiary learning institutions. A SLE is one that features the use of innovative technologies and elements that allow greater flexibility, adaptation, engagement, and feedback for the learner [44]. All in all, these technological advancements are potentially revolutionary for the way teachers and learners interact, paving the way for more learner-centered learning environments. The Smart School is a school that is designed for providing a standard virtual teaching learning environment and as well as improving school management system [45]. The Smart School opens out opportunities and helps all pupils to develop digital skills, creativity and learning to learn. The Smart Schools principles are based on the two guiding beliefs:

- learning is a consequence of thinking, and good thinking is learnable by all students;
- learning should include deep understanding, which involves the flexible, active use of knowledge.

These principles provide a structure for schools with a vision of a learning community that is steeped in thinking and deep understanding, that engenders respect for all its members, and that produces students ready to face the world as responsible, thinking members of a diverse society.

Jen [46] declared five main goals as (1) to provide all-round development of the individual, (2) to provide opportunities to enhance individual strengths and abilities, (3) to produce a thinking and technology-literate workforce, (4) to democratize education, and (5) to increase participation of stakeholders. An appropriate mix of learning strategies is allowed for students to achieve basic competencies and to promote a holistic development. Thus, student-centered learning turns out to be the basis for designing learning activities. High-technology media, such as computer-based teaching-learning materials, the internet, and the World Wide Web, are integrated into conventional media. In order to guarantee the success of the conceptual model of teaching and learning, the Smart Schools require effective and efficient management of the resources and processes to support teaching and learning.

III. HYPOTHESIS AND RESEARCH DESIGN

The case study was investigated in an Italian Middle School (IC3) placed in the City of Modena, composed of 4 different sites distant from each other up to 10 miles (from the central site). Through the Sharp Anywhere· Sharp Anywhere integrates video conferencing with the flexibility of video calling, eliminates the need for meeting rooms and dedicated audio video equipment. It works with a cloud technology.

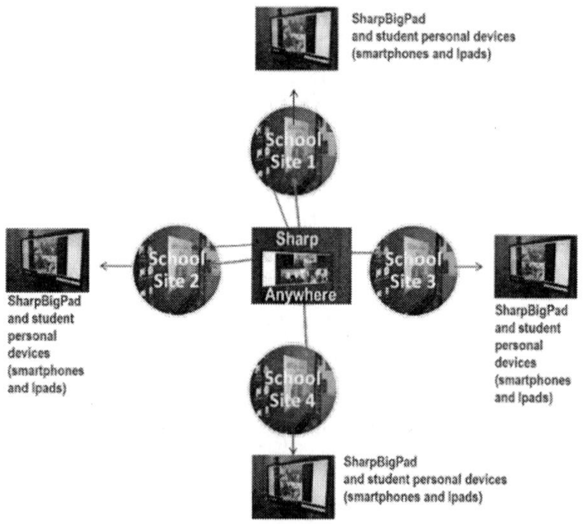

Figure 1. System design: Schools connections and devices.

Sharp has provided 5 BigPad. Sharp BigPad enables the following interactive functions and mobile devices connected via wireless LAN: - sharing of onscreen content; - transfer of files; - interactive onscreen writing and drawing; - remote control from mobile devices.

placed in the classes of different school sites. Mobile BigPad are used in multiple classes Figure 1).

Curricular teachers (n=12) were involved in the disciplinary areas of L1 (Italian Language), Science and Mathematics, Technology and Art. The wireless technology of the BigPad allowed the connection of student devices (smartphone and IPad) with simultaneous sending of photos and digital artifacts of the student's group work.

The Smart School system based on the integration of the tools of GoogleSuite, Sharp Anywhere and Sharp Bigpad was investigated to verify:

- the development of curriculum in soft skills (creativity, teamwork, sense of initiative);
- the methods of conducting the learning environment;
- the development of the idea of professional community and new organizational models of School.

TABLE I. RESEARCH AND METHODOLOGY DESIGN.

People	Age	Meth.	Area	Quant. Tools		Quali. Tools
				Pre	*Post*	*Post*
Stud.	9-12	Exp. n. 96	Creativity Teamwork Self-Direction	Questionnaire (before/after lessons with Sharp BigPad and Sharp Anywhere)		Focus Group
Stud.	9 -12	Trad. n. 85	Creativity Teamwork Self-Direction	Questionnaire (before/after traditional lessons)		-
Teach.	26-58	Exp. n.12	Science Mathematic Italian language Art and Technology	Questionnaire (before/after lessons with Sharp BigPad and design with Sharp Anywhere)		Focus Group
Res. Team		n. 3	Pedagogy Statistic			

The classes involved were five in the experimentation method, and five in control. Mixed method instruments by teachers and students were used: quantitative data were collected through the initial and final questionnaire at the experimental phase (pre-post test) (Table I). For teachers, based on Talis survey, for students, based on European Entrepreneurship Competence Framework (creativity, teamwork, self-direction). Qualitative data were collected through focus groups and in-depth interviews with teachers and students. A research blog for teachers is used as well.

IV. ACTIVITIES

The activities carried out are divided into sex phases:

- phase I: teacher training on Sharp Anywhere and Sharp BigPad (September / October 2017),
- phase II: planning of teaching activities to be carried out in class and planning of teacher support activities (November 2017 / January 2018),
- phase III: initial data collection in the involved classes (experimental and control) and teachers (February 2018),
- phase IV: implementation of teaching activities in classes with Sharp Anywhere and Sharp BigPad and the start of supervision activities for teachers (February / May 2018),
- phase V: final data collection in the involved classes (experimental and control) and teachers (June 2018), phase
- phase VI: dissemination of good practice outcomes, blueprints for the policies, generalization hypothesis (Table II; Table III).

TABLE II. PHASES OF ACTIVITIES.

Phase N.	Sept. 2017	Oct. 2017	Nov. 2017	Dec. 2017	Gen. 2018	Feb. - May 2018
1	Teacher training					
2			Planning teacher activities Planning teacher supervision			
3						Pre test
4						Experimental activities with classes Sharp Bigpad + Anywhere

TABLE III. PHASES OF ACTIVITIES.

Phase N.	Feb. – May 2018	June 2018	July 2018	Aug. 2018
4	Teacher supervision Sharp Anywhere			
5		Post test		
6			Dissemination	

In Phase II and IV, Sharp Anywhere and Sharp BigPad have been used for:

A. *Teachers*

- Connection between different sites to didactic design;
- Connection between teachers and experts outside the school;
- Connection for focus groups and supervision of experimental activities.

Focus Group (FG) is a quality research methodology. The FG is a group interview (with max 10-12 students or teachers) which the researcher asks questions to verify a hypothesis studied with quantitative methods (questionnaires. Usually the FG is played in face-to-face. The Sharp Anywhwere technology has allowed to experiment the FG effectiveness in digital setting.

- Registration and repository the video conferencing in Sharp Anywhere cloud;
- Creation of videoproducts for the continuous training of school teachers and the development of professional communities.

B. *Students*

- Connection between different classes of sites to present learning products;
- Connection between different classes of sites for peer tutoring;
- Connection with classes from other schools for peer tutoring;
- Registration and repository video conferencing of Sharp Anywhere cloud.

Students – as result of cooperative learning work – realized videos to present a topic of lesson at peer students in other site schools (involved into the experimentation). The presentation by BigPad was the opportunity to save the videos into the Anywhere cloud. In this way every school – students and teachers – can "re-use" the videos for learning any time and any where.

- Realization of videoproducts of subjects studied for school database;
- Evaluation of skills based on authentic products.

C. Schools organization

- Connection between different sites for organizational meetings;
- Connection for formal and informal training and information groups;
- Connection for widespread laboratories;
- Connection for parallel classes;
- Connection for staff meetings, team;
- Connection with experts for training and consulting;
- Connection with schools in the training district; Connection for academic lessons.

Some interesting activities were realized with integration of devices. The students working in small groups to produce some artifacts – conceptual maps, new words, concept definition, problem solution – to demonstrate their understanding. With their personal devices, students send the artifacts via wireless on the BigPad and teacher can simultaneously compare the works, debate with classroom, improving deep understanding. The BigPad connected with Sharp Anywhere, saves the students works into "Anywhere cloud" and, in this way, teachers (and schools) build a data base of artifacts (categorized by topic or area of learning). Comparing understanding "just-in-time" and simultaneously – using personal and school devices – improve student's competencies, motivation and engagement (this is teacher observation and consideration during the focus group).

V. CONCLUSION

Through the Sharp Anywhere connection monitoring system, a first partial data shows that the Smart School used 60 hours of teacher-time involved in organizational and training activities. Considering that the time for each teacher dedicated from the work contract to the didactic planning is 30 hours, a first result in the Smart School shows how there has been an extension of the planning time with a reduction of the movement time from site to site (Figure 2).

As a consequence, the School technological devices increases the availability of teachers, an optimization of work-time and a possible higher quality of school time.

A second consideration shows how on-demand supervision activities were possible - anywhere and anytime with personal devices (smartphones and IPads) - strengthening the idea of the professional learning community, and outlining the figure of the in-service educational supervisor. This aspect answers the questions emerging in modern teacher education related at the quality of teaching and learning [47][48].

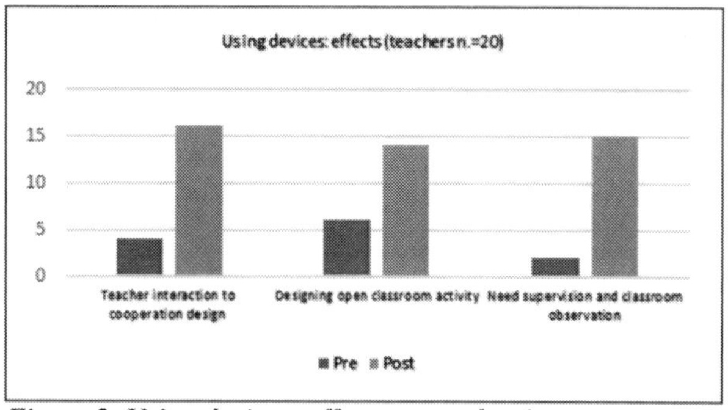

Figure 2. Using devices: effects on teacher into experimental design.

A third consideration concerns the extension of the possibilities for the qualitative research methodology: it is now possible in the Smart School the realization of quality focus groups through the integration of tools, such as Sharp Anywhere and Sharp BigPad, with digital environments for research and continuing education.

A fourth consideration is emerging from focus groups (Table IV): teachers refer the engagement in new didactic methodology and peer collaboration to sustain a professional learning community. The education video production during video supervision – with Sharp Anywhere and Sharp BigPad – is a "cloud resource" to enhance competencies and lifelong learner profile. Cooperative Learning method is used to engage students into project work and to delivery with wireless line, by smartphones, products and learning objects into BigPad.

TABLE IV. RESULTS OF TEACHER FOCUS GROUP.

Strengths	**Weaknesses**
To use personal devices for learning Student motivation Student engagement Student cooperation Student deep understanding Student creativity Teacher support (supervision) Improving quality of pedagogy Improving school climate and quality of teacher work	Short time of experience Few colleagues involved
Opportunities	**Threats**
To realize video for learning To realize school cloud for learning To realize opportunity to share knowledge To build Smart School	No continuity of experience Opposition to change school organization Opposition to culture of innovation

REFERENCES

[1] OECD-PISA, "The PISA 2012 Technical Report", Paris, OECD Publishing, 2014.

[2] IEA, "TIMSS and PIRLS 2011: Relationships Among Reading, Mathematics, and Science Achievement at the

Fourth Grade - Implications for Early Learning", Chestnut Hill, MA, TIMSS & PIRLS International Study Center, Boston College, 2013.

[3] OECD-TALIS, "TALIS 2103 Results. An International Perspective on Teaching and Learning", Paris, OECD, 2013.

[4] OECD-TALIS, "Creating Effective Teaching and Learning Environments: First Results from TALIS", Paris, OECD Publishing, 2009.

[5] Eurydice, "The Teaching Profession in Europe: Practices, Perceptions, and Policies", Eurydice Report, Luxembourg, European Union Publications, 2015.

[6] OECD, "Education at a Glance 2014", Paris, OECD Publishing, 2014.

[7] J. A. C. Hattie, "Visible learning. A synthesis of over 800 meta analyses relating to achievement", New York, Routledge, 2009.

[8] J. A. C. Hattie, "Visible learning for teachers", New York, Routledge, 2012.

[9] J. D. Bransford, A. L. Brown and R. R. Cocking, "How people learn: brain, mind, experience, and school", Washington, DC, National Academy Press, 2000.

[10] F. Benavides, H. Dumont, and D. Instance, "Innovative learning environment". In CERI-OCSE, Innovating to Learn. Learning to Innovate. Bologna: Il Mulino, 2011.

[11] Y. Engeström, "Expansive learning at work: Toward an activity theoretical reconceptualization", Journal of Education and Work, vol. 14, pp. 133-156, 2001.

[12] L. S. Vygotskij, "Thought and language", Cambridge, MIT, 1962.

[13] J. Bruner, "The culture of education", New York, Norton, 1966.

[14] A. L. Brown, "The Advancement of Learning", Educational Researcher, vol. 23, n.8, pp. 4-12, 1994.

[15] U. Margiotta, "The structure of cognitive modificability: a new deal for education in the XXI Age", in (Ed.) U. Margiotta, "The changing mind. From Neural plasticity to cognitive modifiability", Lecce, Pensa Multimedia, 2011.

[16] R. Feuerstein, "The Theory of Structural Cognitive Modifiability", in (Ed.) B. Presseisen, "Learning and thinking styles: classroom instruction", Washington, National Education Association Rsearch for Better Schools, 1990.

[17] G. Rizzolatti and C. Sinigaglia, "I know what you do. The brain that acts and the mirror neurons", Milano, RaffaelloCortina, 2006.

[18] L. Craighero, "The mirrors neurons", Bologna: Il Mulino, 2010.

[19] V. Gallese, "At the origin of the interaction with others. Society and individuals", vol. 35, n. 2, pp. 115-124, 2009.

[20] G. Lakoff and R. E. Nunez, "Where does math come from? How the embodied mind originates the mathematics", Torino, Bollati Boringhieri, 2005.

[21] L. Cozolino, "The social brain. Neurosciences of human relationships", Milano, Raffaello Cortina, 2008.

[22] OECD-CERI, "The nature of learning: Using research to inspire practice", p. 69-90, Paris, OECD Publishing, 2010.

[23] Europe Union, "Efficiency and equity in European education and training systems", Bruxelles, Comunicazione commissione, 2006.

[24] DeSeCo-OECD, "DeSeCo: theoretical and comceptual foundations. Strategy paper", Neushatel, OECD Publishing, 2002.

[25] J. Huber and P. Mompoint-Guillard, "Teacher education for change", Strasburgo, Consiglio d'Europa, 2011.

[26] I. Zitter and A. Hoeve, "Hybrid Learning Environments: Merging Learning and Work Processes to Facilitate Knowledge Integration and Transitions", OECD Education Working Papers, No. 81, OECD Publishing, 2012.

[27] J. Manninen et al., "Environments that Support Learning: An Introduction to the Learning Environments Approach", Finnish National Board of Education, Helsinki, 2007.

[28] P. Goodyear, "Effective Networked Learning in Higher Education: Notes and Guidelines", Lancaster University, 2001.

[29] A. Schleicher, (Ed.) "Preparing Teachers and Developing School Leaders for the 21st Century", Brussels, OECD Publishing, 2012.

[30] J. Mezirow, "Transformative dimensions of adult learning", San Francisco, Jossey-Bass, 1991.

[31] D. A. Kolb, "Experiential Learning: experience as the source of learning and development", New J, Prentice-Hall, 1984.

[32] M. Knowles, "Andragogy in Action", San Francisco, Jossey-Bass, 1994

[33] D. Schön, "The reflective practitioner", NY, Basic Books, 1993.

[34] L. Darling-Hammond, R. Chung Wei, A. Andree, R. Richardson and S. Orphanos, "Professional Learning in the learning profession", Dallas, TX, NSDC, 2009.

[35] R. DuFour and R. Eaker, "Professional learning communities at work: Best practices for enhancing student achievement", Bloomington, IA, National Education Service, 1998.

[36] M. A. Fullen and J. A. Catt, J.A., "Soil Management: Problems and Solutions", London, Arnold, 2004.

[37] S. M. Hord, "Professional learning communities: An overview", In (Ed.) S. Hord "Learning together, leading together: Changing schools through professional learning communities", New York, Teachers College Press, 2004.

[38] P. M. Senge, et al. "Schools that learn: A fifth discipline fieldbook for educators, parents and everyone who cares about education", New York, Currency-Doubleday, 2000.

[39] M. Morrisey, "Professional learning communities: An ongoing exploration", Austin, TX, Southwest Educational Development Laboratory, 2000.

[40] C. Murphy and D. Lick, "Whole-faculty study groups: Creating professional learning communities that target student learning", Thousand Oaks, CA, Corwin Press, 2004.

[41] S. M. Hord and W. A. Sommers, Leading Professional Learning Community, Thousands Oaks, CA, CorvinPress, 2008.

[42] R. DuFour, "Schools as Learning Communities", Educational Leadership, vol.61, n.8, pp. 6-11, 2004.

[43] S. Zepeda, "Professional development: what works, Larchmont, NY, Eye on Education, 2008.

[44] J. M. Spector, "Conceptualizing the emerging field of smart learning environments", Smart Learning Environments, vol. 1, n.2, 2014, http://slejournal.springeropen.com/articles/10.1186/s40561-014-0002-7 (retrieved: may, 2018).

[45] UNESCO, "In Pursuit of Smart Learning Environments for the 21st Century", In-Progress Reflection, n.12, July, 2017.

[46] I. Chin and J. Chia-Sen "Application of the Concepts of the Smart Schools of Malaysia to Taiwan's Technology Education" https://www.iteea.org/File.aspx?id=80246&v=ba6064fd (retrieved: may, 2018).

[47] L. Darling-Hammond, "Strengthening Clinical Preparation: The Holy Grail of Teacher Education", Peabody Journal of Education, vol. 89, n. 4, pp. 547-561, 2014.

[48] COM, "Supporting the Teaching Professions for Better Learning Outcomes", Brussels, European Commission, 2013.